## Additional Praise for *Understanding Bible by Design*

"Don't worry if you are new to the notion of course design, backward design, or understanding by design. If you care about teaching and want to do more than just tweak your syllabi, this exciting volume is for you. Lester, Webster, and Jones offer practical advice on designing courses that reflect your true learning objectives. Intended specifically for biblical studies professors, *Understanding Bible by Design* far surpasses any one-size-fits-all workshop or professional development seminar on pedagogy. It provides clear, helpful, and user-friendly guidance on designing and implementing innovative teaching in diverse learning environments."

**Nyasha Junior**
**Howard University School of Divinity**

"This book is a must-buy for the Wabash Center's library. It's not a tips and tricks book. Instead, it's an entire approach to course design and assessment in quick accessible prose. The opening chapter provides a concise overview of Wiggins and McTighe's *Understanding by Design*. Subsequent chapters illustrate this method at work through hands-on examples from the design of a real-life biblical studies course. This process is then repeated for an online course, a college level liberal arts course, and for courses outside of biblical studies. The book walks us through the essential questions to ask when designing a course. What is most important for students to learn? What student performance would provide evidence of this learning? And what activities or assignments would help students develop these skills? It's easy! And a pleasure to read."

**Thomas Pearson**
**Wabash Center for Teaching and Learning**
**in Theology and Religion**

"Lester and his colleagues explain in clear, engaging terms why professors of biblical studies should invest the time to explore backward course design. Using detailed examples grounded in their own teaching practice, they invite careful attention to focusing on what really matters to enhance student learning. With their fingers on the pulse of contemporary teaching challenges such as multiple time formats and new environments for course delivery, they serve as creative collaborators and guides for both novice and veteran teachers in the field."

**Katherine Turpin**
**Iliff School of Theology**

# Understanding Bible by Design
## Create Courses with Purpose

### G. Brooke Lester

*with*

Jane S. Webster
Christopher M. Jones

UNDERSTANDING BIBLE BY DESIGN
Create Courses with Purpose

Cover image: yganko/iStock/Thinkstock
Cover design: Laurie Ingram
Book design: PerfecType, Nashville, TN

*Library of Congress Cataloging-in-Publication Data is available*
Print ISBN: 978-1-4514-8879-1
eBook ISBN: 978-1-4514-8962-0

The paper used in this publication meets the minimum requirements of American National Standard for Information Sciences — Permanence of Paper for Printed Library Materials, ANSI Z329.48-1984.

Manufactured in the U.S.A.

# Contents

**1** Setting the Problem

*G. Brooke Lester* ...................................................................... 1

**2** Understanding by Design

*G. Brooke Lester* ...................................................................... 9

**3** Understanding by Design: Old Testament in Seminary

*G. Brooke Lester* .................................................................... 33

**4** Understanding by Design: Putting Your Course Online

*G. Brooke Lester* .................................................................... 61

**5** Understanding by Design: New Testament at University

*Jane S. Webster* ..................................................................... 71

Exhibit 3: Annotated Sample Template for Essay in "New Testament"

*Jane S. Webster* ..................................................................... 82

**6** Understanding by Design: Judaism Studies at University

*Christopher M. Jones* ............................................................. 97

## Appendix

Exhibit 1: Rubric for Presentations

*G. Brooke Lester* .................................................................. 118

Exhibit 2: All-Purpose Rubric for "Introduction to the Old Testament"

*G. Brooke Lester* .................................................................. 119

**Exhibit 4: Interdisciplinary Institutional Rubric for Writing at Barton College**

*Jane S. Webster* ............................................................ 120

**Exhibit 5: Rubric for Essays in "New Testament"**

*Jane S. Webster* ............................................................ 121

**Exhibit 6: Rubric for Ritual Analysis Papers in "Ritual and Ritualization"**

*Christopher M. Jones*..................................................... 123

**Exhibit 7: Rubric for Drafts in "Space and Place in Early Jewish Literature"**

*Christopher M. Jones*..................................................... 124

## Chapter 1

# Setting the Problem

G. *Brooke Lester*

T his is a book about Understanding by Design (UbD), and how some of us have used it to design our courses in biblical studies better. UbD, developed by Grant Wiggins and Jay McTighe, is a teacher-friendly, learner-centered approach to "backward course design," by which one builds a course "backward," using the destination—one's desired learning outcomes—as a starting place.

Recently, at my own institution, a few junior faculty members advanced a plan for a faculty forum in which they might elicit insights from professional educators and senior faculty members about how to accomplish more intelligent course design. A senior faculty member, speaking in support of the idea, remarked that he was intrigued because, as he said, "It would never have occurred to me that anybody would 'design' a course."

"Course design" may be a subject you feel you have beaten your head against already, or the concept may strike you as novel. But if you like the idea of creating and revising your religious-studies courses with a plan and a clarity of purpose, then this book is for you.

## "I Don't Know How You Do It"

It was my own personal *Groundhog Day*.[1]

"I'm revising my 'Intro' syllabus again," I announced, with a forced bravado that I could tell did not disguise a substantial substrate of chagrin.

---

*http://www.ascd.org/research-a-topic/understanding-by-design-resources.aspx

1. In this movie (Columbia Pictures, 1993), the protagonist is forced to re-live the same day, hundreds of times, until he Learns a Valuable Lesson.

1

My conversation partner would shake her head. "That's laudable. Why?" After listening patiently through my recital, she would carefully not quite ask, "What's in it for you?" Instead, she would fall back on pointed "I" statements: "I don't know how you do it. I would never get my committee work/journal article/reports/peer reviews finished if I revised my syllabi every year as you do." *Tell me about it*, I would carefully not quite say.

In one iteration, I was changing the textbook, in search of something less overtly in the Protestant confessional scholarly tradition (*"The old textbook essentializes Canaanites in a way that goes beyond evidence and fosters Christian triumphalist essentializing of Judaism!"*). In another, I was dropping an older assignment to make room for a Wikipedia-editing project (*"Public biblical scholars!"*). In yet another, I was experimenting with a less draconian, more negotiable late-work policy (*"Adult learners!"*). In the next, I was changing the textbook again.

The thing is, there usually *was* something in it for me: rescuing myself from the intractable problems generated by the *previous* revision. The new textbook solved the Canaanite problem, but barely nodded to the possibility of substantive religious and social diversity in its readership. The Wikipedia project worked wonders with the students who did it, but involved a substantive temporal investment in becoming acquainted with Wikipedia's guidelines for editing. The late-work policy solved the "empty-threat" problem (ever try to enforce no-late-work-accepted when one-third of the assignments drift in past deadline?), but added three pages of legalese to a syllabus already swollen well into "tl;dr" territory ("too long; didn't read"). Every revision served a double purpose: to try something new to make *Something Happen* (more learner engagement, better quiz results, dynamic discussions, higher enrollment . . .), and to save myself from the agonies of the last revision.

My colleague and I are both stuck in our respective loops. For her, the loop is simply to live with the dissatisfactions of her course . . . for good reasons. For me, the loop is to hack term by term without a plan . . . for my own good reasons. Both of us would appear, to a hypothetical observer with a clue, to be in need of an intervention.

Against popular belief, I am given to understand that neither Albert Einstein, nor Mark Twain, nor Ben Franklin actually ever said, "The definition of insanity is to do the same thing over and over again while always expecting different results."[2] And, the witticism doesn't stand up to even a cursory knowledge of mental illness. Nonetheless, whoever did say it was a regular Einstein.

I thought that I needed some tweak, or combination of tweaks, that I just hadn't yet discovered. And—*obviously!*—that tweak would involve some magical assembly of just the right resources and activities. After all, what else is there? Learners read/view/hear stuff, and they do stuff. It's just a matter of finding the Right Stuff. What I actually needed was to be told that the resources and activities *weren't the problem and didn't matter*.

---

2. The earliest versions of the statement appear to arise in addictions-recovery circles, http://www.news .hypercrit.net/2012/11/13/einstein-on-misattribution-i-probably-didnt-say-that/.

Hard to hear, right? Because, if you are like most of us in biblical studies, a "course" is defined by that syllabus—that collection of resources, activities, and policies—that you inherited from your mentors and have fiddled with ever since, from small changes to whole rewrites. And that won't get anywhere. To understand why that's hard to hear, you need to know what happened when my laptop battery almost went dead while I drafted this chapter in my office, having left my charger at home.

## A Designer's-Eye View

I went downstairs to cadge a charger off the IT people, and the Database Admin (DBA) was complaining casually about an encounter she had had with an employee in one of the offices. This employee habitually engaged in some practice that caused havoc in the DBA's computer environment (possibly making overly large databases). The employee repeatedly called upon the DBA to fix the problem, but he refused to hear that his practices *were* the problem. His repeated chorus was, "Make things so that I can work the way I habitually work, without things going wrong." The DBA's repeated response was, "You are the reason things go wrong. I can teach you a different way to do your task—the right way—such that things don't go wrong."

A medical professional looks tiredly at his patient. The patient wants to know how she can keep providing for her family while doing her job at the same hours and in the same ways that she currently does it. The medical professional, without much hope, explains that what the patient is doing is what's making her sick.

These episodes plays out in every workplace, whether a corporate cubicle farm, a manufacturing plant, or an institution of higher education. Especially acute are the situations where the expert does not possess the actual authority to enforce her prescriptions, and where the boss (to whom both parties answer) fails to support her (which he could do by saying, "Hey, I pay this DBA for a reason; do what she says, or her paycheck might as well be going out the window!").

So it is, frequently, with the course designer (if your institution is fortunate to have a course designer) or with those few higher-ed instructors with an educational background in pedagogy. Instructors want advice about how to get better results with the resources and activities that they habitually include in their courses (hey, there's my colleague in the anecdote that begins this chapter), or at most want to hear what "fresh" resources and activities might solve the problems that they face each term (and there's me!). But it's hard for us to hear that the resources and activities aren't the real problem. As is always the case when parties are talking past one another, there is a clash of presuppositions here: the instructor assumes that "resources and activities" are the *heart* of the course, whereas the course designer sees "resources and activities" as replaceable modules. So where, for the designer, is the heart of the course? The heart of the course is in its learning outcomes: When a learner completes the course, what things, *specifically*, ought she to understand and to be able to do?

## Dreams and Gripes (Or, A Funny Thing Happened on My Way to Damascus)

For me, the scales-from-the-eyes moment came as I worked through a four-week assignment in course design, as part of my work in a certification program in online pedagogy. Having chosen a lesson or unit (for example, "The Writings" as one unit in "Introduction to the Hebrew Bible/Old Testament"), we designed our lessons in four stages. The assignment did not incorporate UbD, but was a more basic example of Backward Course Design.

In Stage One, we created a "learner profile," and identified three or more "lesson topics" (tasks or concepts to be learned). For example, a topic might be a course unit like "Pentateuch" or "Writings," or a more focused topic like "History of the People Israel" or "Ideological Criticism."

In Stage Two, we used those topics as the basis for "learning objectives," or "outcomes of significance," built using verbs associated with Bloom's (revised) taxonomy:[3] "Upon completion of this unit, learners will be able to . . . (define, describe, predict, analyze, create, assess, etc.)." For example, the topic "History of the People Israel" may give rise to a learning objective like, "Learners will be able to describe the difference between the world 'in' a biblical text and the world 'behind' that biblical text."[4] The topic "Ideological Criticism" may prompt something like, "Learners will be able to analyze a given biblical text in terms of its worldview and the rhetorical strategies by which it seeks to reproduce that worldview in the reader." As will be seen in the next chapter, the concept of "big ideas and essential questions" would be a helpful bridge between these first two stages. Lying behind the learning objectives given here, one might find big ideas like "Academic biblical studies differs from confessional 'Bible study' in its presuppositions and participants," or "A text doesn't have one 'correct' meaning to be found out but, rather, a constantly evolving range of supportable meanings always being contributed to."

In Stage Three, we turned our "learning objectives" into an assessment rubric, writing descriptions of what a learner's performance for each objective would look like if its performance were unsatisfactory, minimal, accomplished, or exemplary. This is the step most unintuitive for many instructors: writing an assessment rubric for learning objectives that are *not yet associated with any particular activities or resources*. But stop a moment, and think about how you actually talk about student work: in terms of your greatest dreams and most irritated complaints. For most of us, these dreams and gripes are not too hard for us, or too far away. They aren't in heaven, that we would have to ask who will go up and get them for us, or across the sea, that we need to ask someone to cross over and bring them. Dreams and gripes are *ready to hand*. They are honed to specificity through years of repetition (in carefully controlled prose) in the margins of papers and (in more unfiltered

---

3. On Bloom's Taxonomy and its revision, see, for example, Richard C. Overbaugh and Lynn Schultz, "Bloom's Taxonomy," http://ww2.odu.edu/educ/roverbau/Bloom/blooms_taxonomy.htm.

4. This way of distinguishing between biblical narrative and the real-world history giving rise to biblical texts I owe to Terence E. Fretheim, Gene M. Tucker, and Charles B. Cousar, *The Pentateuch*, Interpreting Biblical Texts (Nashville: Abingdon, 1996), 22–36.

form) by the coffeemaker in the faculty lounge. Peruse your comments on relevant past student work and you can quickly find your language for the "unsatisfactory" column of your rubric. Glance over your swollen syllabus and assignment descriptions, in which you describe at ever-greater length your aspirations for student performance, and there's fodder for your "exemplary" column. Then the die is cast, and you can do your provisional work on describing the "good-enough-but-not-great" range in the two middle columns (or, if it's easier, collapse these into a single "good-enough" middle column).[5]

Only in Stage Four did we finally get into resources and activities. We wrote up an "instructional strategy" for our lesson or unit: a cycle of elements such as lecture, readings, or other self-directed learning, discussion, projects, case studies, and so forth. For each element, we were to list (1) the learning objectives addressed by the element, (2) how we would explain the element to our learners, and (3) what activities the learners would undertake to accomplish the element.

The first "scales-falling-from-eyes" aspect of this for me was the realization that *selecting resources and activities became trivial*. With a destination clearly mapped out in the learning outcomes and assessment rubrics, my habitual resources and activities virtually lined up to be included or discarded, very much like a scarf suggests itself for a February trip to the grocery store, whereas a pair of swimming flippers—however expensive or ingeniously designed—suggests itself for exclusion.

The second "scales-falling-from-eyes" aspect of this for me was the realization that *environment didn't matter*. If I chose "lecture," or a "collaborative project," it was because I felt that this was the best way to address a particular learning objective. If the course was face-to-face, or online, or in a bathysphere at the bottom of the sea, then making the activity work in that environment was just a matter of logistics.

I felt light-footed and free.

I discovered Understanding by Design in a flurry of enthusiastic research following this project. If the above assignment felt like someone allowing in a sliver of light to illuminate the troubles I had had during my long dark night of course design and redesign, then UbD was like someone kicking in the door and waving me into the daylight.

## What Every Grown-up Already Knows about "Backward" Design

It's not that I had never heard the admonishment, "Build your course backward from your learning goals." It's just that it sounded (and seemed, in my limited practice) really artificial and abstruse.

You know what doesn't sound really artificial and abstruse? This: "Know where you want to go before you plan how to get there."

I remember the first time I encountered the mantra that, when developing or revising a course, we "start with learning outcomes." I would try to do so, with moderate success, though I tended to focus on knowledge ("They should know

---

5. This approach to constructing rubrics is excellently described in a work I recommend highly, Dannelle D. Stevens and Antonia Levi, *Introduction to Rubrics: An Assessment Tool to Save Grading Time, Convey Effective Feedback, and Promote Student Learning*, 1st ed. (Sterling, VA: Stylus, 2005).

the history of Israel from the Merneptah Stele through 164 BCE") to the exclusion of other aspects of understanding (in UbD terms, *explanation, interpretation, application, perspective, empathy, self-knowledge*). But while I could generate learning outcomes in a general and ad hoc way, hooking these reflections into the course design itself was something I couldn't wrap my mind around. Working "backward" just seemed so . . . backward.

Consider the winter errand I alluded to briefly above, however: when deciding between an umbrella, a sun hat, and a scarf, we all acknowledge that, practically speaking, one's destination doesn't conclude a winter errand, it begins it. Anyone who has successfully managed a project or planned an expedition already has an intuitive understanding of "backward" design.

Many project managers are already familiar with David Allen's well-known "Getting Things Done" (GTD) approach to project management.[6] As he says, a project begins with a statement of "purposes and principles" behind the project: Why are we doing this project? What makes it important? (For example, "Little Zoey tripped in the dark in the garage and skinned her hands. A well-lit and clean garage is safer for my family than a dark and cluttered garage.") Having established the purposes and principles driving the project, it's time to *start at the end*, with an outcome that can be envisioned. What, in detail, are the features of a well-lit and uncluttered garage? What evidence, in detail, would constitute a satisfactory demonstration that my garage is well lit and uncluttered? Only then are you in a position to brainstorm ideas ("In no particular order, what is involved in cleaning and lighting the garage?"), organizing ("What orderings are logically required to manage these steps sensibly?"), and identifying next actions ("What comes first?"). Having worked *backward* from a carefully envisioned outcome, we arrive—at the *end* of our planning—at the beginning, our first step.

Also familiar with "backward" design is anyone who has planned, say, a backpacking trip or any other expedition. It's trivial to point out that, in this example, you have to know your literal destination before you can plan your route. Going further, you will want to know the conditions under which you will be making the journey (Will water be plentiful and temperatures low, as in June, or water scarce and temps high, as in August?), and the analogy to learning environments readily suggests itself (Are we face-to-face or online? If online, asynchronously or synchronously? In an open or closed system?). But I will go even one step further: when planning a trip, you don't just want to know the literal destination and conditions; you want to know *what you want participants to get out of the journey*. Do I want my twelve-year-old to feel the bracing rewards of covering long miles, or am I trying to seduce him into the backpacking lifestyle with scenic vistas and long afternoons enjoying activities around camp? Does my partner look forward to the challenges of outdoor cooking and cleaning, or, rather, to my having relieved her of these tasks because this is, after all, vacation? Even on this kind of entirely nonmetaphorical "journey," there are more destinations at play than the literal port of call.

---

6. David Allen, *Getting Things Done: The Art of Stress-Free Productivity* (New York: Viking, 2001), 13–14, 56.

## When All Else Fails, Read the Instructions

Let's face a couple of hard facts: time invested in course (re)design pays few direct rewards in higher education, and—given our own professional preparation as biblical scholars—most of us aren't already good enough at it to manage it efficiently, left to our own devices.

Time invested in course design has only the most indirect consequences for job security, promotion, and tenure. At most institutions, student course evaluations (sometimes called "customer satisfaction surveys" by weary instructors) and GPAs serve as the most weighty indicators of teaching effectiveness. If you talk a lot about your course (re)designs, some colleague on a promotion committee may (*may!*) raise the point in your favor. But this speculative possibility is a thin reed on which to lean. So, where is the payoff for time invested in course design? The anecdote with which I started this chapter suggests its negative formulation: I hope that each redesign helps me waste less time and have fewer bad experiences with learners. Let's put that, then, more positively: *Time invested in course design can result in net savings of time spent teaching and assessing, and can set the stage for more good experiences with learners.*

So, the motivation is there. Yet, as surprising as it might seem to all those regular people who don't live and breathe and have their being in academia, our familiarity with "education" as a field of study varies staggeringly. In my own PhD program, a student could find opportunity to do several semesters of teaching fellowships, each involving several hours of independent time with groups of learners. However, our exposure to pedagogical theory and the history of education as a discipline was limited to a single, one-day workshop . . . and this, for most of us, *after* our teaching fellowships were behind us. At the institution where I teach now, PhD students (before they begin serving as teaching assistants) all take a three-credit-hour January "intensive" teaching seminar. A very few have degrees specifically in education. True, the move toward online learning has prompted a kind of renaissance for pedagogy in institutions of higher education, as schools are forced to make public claims about what specific features of their online offerings make them as good as traditional face-to-face offerings. For example, many faculty members at my school have earned professional certificates in online teaching, involving course work that emphasizes constructivist learning, collaborative learning, "backward course design," learner-centered instruction, performance-based assessment, the flipped classroom, and other critical issues and conversation pieces in contemporary pedagogy. Nonetheless, such programs are recent and not all instructors willingly embrace them. Frequently, little or nothing is offered in the way of course relief or committee relief to compensate for the added attention to pedagogy, and many instructors understandably "beg off" of such professional development if allowed. Recent trends notwithstanding, the pedagogical foundations on which higher-ed instructors build and renovate our courses is distressingly uneven, and with our varied backgrounds, our conversations are a babel of different pedagogical languages, spoken with varying levels of literacy.

However much teaching sits most obviously among the "holy trinity" of teaching, service, and scholarship, the fact is that, as a class, many teachers have only uneven grounding in the scholarship of teaching and learning. However motivated we are to reap the benefits of more efficient, outcomes-based course design, we are largely without understanding. We need a plan.

We need UbD.

## Works Cited

Allen, David. *Getting Things Done: The Art of Stress-Free Productivity*. New York: Viking, 2001.

Becker, Michael. "Einstein on Misattribution: 'I Probably Didn't Say That.'" http://www.news.hypercrit.net/2012/11/13/einstein-on-misattribution-i-probably-didnt-say-that/.

Fretheim, Terence E., Gene M. Tucker, and Charles B. Cousar. *The Pentateuch*. Interpreting Biblical Texts. Nashville: Abingdon, 1996.

Overbaugh, Richard C. and Lynn Schultz, "Bloom's Taxonomy," http://ww2.odu.edu/educ/roverbau/Bloom/blooms_taxonomy.htm.

Stevens, Dannelle D., and Antonia Levi. *Introduction to Rubrics: An Assessment Tool to Save Grading Time, Convey Effective Feedback, and Promote Student Learning*. 1st ed. Sterling, VA: Stylus, 2005.

## Chapter 2

# Understanding by Design

*G. Brooke Lester*

I n this chapter, I describe Understanding by Design (UbD), as developed by Grant Wiggins and Jay McTighe, but through a "biblical-studies" lens. What is UbD, when did it come along, who uses it, and what does it offer to the instructor in Bible?

## Origins, Publication, and Reception of UbD

"Understanding by Design," as already noted, is a concept developed by Grant Wiggins and Jay McTighe. The first edition of their book *Understanding by Design* was published in 1998, with an accompanying handbook following in 1999. The *Understanding by Design Professional Development Workbook* was released in 2004, shortly before the second, expanded edition of *Understanding By Design* emerged in 2005.[1]

In the UbD model of course design, course units are constructed in three stages. First, the instructor specifies the desired results: What understandings is the learner expected to develop? Second, one determines "acceptable evidence": What will the learner need to perform in order to demonstrate the knowledge and skills desired? Third, one plans the instruction itself: What resources and activities will

---

*http://www.ascd.org/publications/books/103055/chapters/Understanding-Understanding.aspx

1. Grant P. Wiggins and Jay McTighe, *Understanding by Design*, exp. 2nd ed. (Alexandria, VA: Association for Supervision and Curriculum Development, 2005). Grant P. Wiggins and Jay McTighe; idem, *Understanding by Design Professional Development Workbook* (Alexandria, VA: Association for Supervision and Curriculum Development, 2004).

prepare the learner to accomplish the performances that will provide evidence of understanding?

UbD is oriented toward the *learning units that make up a course.* For example, an "Introduction to Hebrew Bible" course might include canonical units (say, Torah, Former Prophets, Latter Prophets, Writings), or a series of historical units (e.g., premonarchy, united monarchy, divided kingdoms, etc.), or thematic units (genre and contexts, ancient Near Eastern comparative literature, gender and nationality in the Bible). UbD is not a recipe for session planning—though session planning falls readily into place once we know our plan for the learning unit of which the session is a part. UbD is not a program for curriculum, but provides a model that can inform curriculum design and revision.[2]

Understanding by Design has enjoyed a strong, positive reception. Its developers are most closely involved in the K–12 world, and there especially UbD has been widely adopted. The world of higher education has been slower to adopt UbD, not because of resistance, but because "course design" does not have the same attention in higher ed as in K–12: instructors in higher ed (I think I can justify this sweeping generalization) are seen less as professional educators and more as content masters who educate. This is changing rapidly, though. The adoption of online and blended/hybrid learning models in higher education have prompted the colleges, universities, and seminaries to rethink and rearticulate their presuppositions about what learning is and how it happens, not only to teach effectively, but also to justify their online/blended programs to the public and to their accrediting agencies. Pedagogy is "in" as it hasn't been before, especially in the growing number of certification programs in online learning. Along with increased attention to learning theories (e.g., constructivism, connectionism) and to teaching practices (e.g., the flipped classroom), we see in higher education ever more interest in course design, especially UbD.

## The Three Stages of UbD

**Stage One:** Identify Desired Results.

*What are the understandings that a student should gain as a result of participation?*

**Stage Two:** Determine Acceptable Evidence.

*What performances would provide compelling evidence that a learner has gained the understandings desired?*

**Stage Three:** Plan Learning Experiences and Instruction.

*What resources and activities are available that can prepare the learner to accomplish the necessary performances?*

---

2. Wiggins and McTighe, *Understanding by Design,* ch. 12; and idem, *Understanding by Design Professional Development Workbook,* 19–22.

In practice, this is an iterative rather than linear process.[3] For example, creating assessment rubrics in the second stage may prompt the instructor to rethink and revise her desired outcomes. Still, the model is teleological in its structure: resources and activities are chosen with the *goal* of preparing the student to succeed in her performances, and those performances are devised with the *goal* of providing clear evidence of the desired understandings. These understandings are articulated to work in service to a manageable set of "big ideas," explicitly pertaining to the subject matter and available to the learners.

Is this "teaching to the test"? It is, but not "tests" limited to closed-ended, forced-choice assessments that demonstrate test-taking skills and the recollection of right answers better than they show genuine understanding. Here, "test" would include more products or performances that the student constructs in response to open-ended prompts reflecting real-world situations.

## Stage One: Identifying Desired Results

In order to identify what "understandings" we want learners to arrive at in the course of a learning unit, we will need to examine what we mean by "understanding," and generate such "big ideas and essential questions" as animate our own urgency, as instructors, about the course and its units.

### *Some Deck-Clearing Convictions about "Understanding"*

Understanding by Design sees "understanding" as complex, or pluriform: there are many ways to understand, described by UbD in terms of six "facets" of understanding. UbD's "Six Facets of Understanding," described below, are first introduced in light of some explicit presuppositions about the nature of understanding:[4]

*Understanding goes beyond recall.* Think, for example, of the student who can rattle off accurate data about years on the Hebrew Bible timeline, but cannot yet use that date to respond to any actual questions (except, say, "What happened around 922 BCE?"). As Wiggins and McTighe put it, it's not enough to recall the facts or approaches that you've been taught; one must be able to "use them *mindfully*." Those familiar with Bloom's revised taxonomy may recall (see what I did there?) its distinction between "remembering" and "understanding" (originally "knowledge" and "comprehension"). Each of the "Six Facets of Understanding" reflect some aspect of "using [recalled facts or approaches] mindfully." Recollection is static: the learner remembers something, or does not. "Use" is dynamic: the learner takes action, making judgments, attempting to put remembered information to use. If a learner is asked to describe the different contexts of Isaiah of Jerusalem and Second Isaiah, and *draws on* her recollection of the timeline to construct an answer (722, 701, 586, 539 BCE), then she could be said to be using recalled facts mindfully.

---

3. Wiggins and McTighe, *Understanding by Design*, 7; and idem, *Understanding by Design Professional Development Handbook*, 4, 25–26.
4. Wiggins and McTighe, *Understanding by Design*, 35–55.

*Understanding involves transfer.* A learner grasps that the biblical Wisdom literature reflects competing perspectives on God's nature and activity in the world, then rings changes on that insight to ask perceptive questions about, say, different, competing theological outlooks among the biblical prophets, or (in a different course) among the heresy debates in the early church. Understanding is apparent where a student can select from among a body of learned facts, discerning which may be relevant for application to a novel situation. This goes beyond an artificial, fill-in-the-blanks "plugging in" of facts. Rather, the learner is able to take some idea about which she has come to some understanding in a certain area, and can "modify, adjust, and adapt" it for use elsewhere.[5] Readers familiar with recent conversations about "hacking" as learning will appreciate this expression of transferability: you understand something if you can "hack on it," make it your own for your own reasons. Experience with hacking on previous learning is one big step toward lifelong learning.

*Understanding is not coverage.* Wiggins and McTighe call this the "expert blind spot."[6] Readers may be familiar with the now-common distinction between "teacher-centered" instruction and "learner-centered" instruction. Instructor's convictions about "what I need" in order to teach a course often revolve around the need for *coverage.* In the often-heard teacher's refrain that "we need to cover" the textbook, the history of Israel, the historical movements of biblical studies, the critical issues, and so forth, we observe the "expert blind spot": the expert's eye sees the many details embraced by the subject matter, but does not see the crucial element of *relevance.* If these details find no relevance in a context comprehensible to the learner, she won't have anything to do with them. (On reflection, I mean that last phrase in both senses: she won't have any application ready-to-hand by which the facts can "sink in" through use, and also, she is likely to reject their importance outright, and who can blame her?) If we are honest with ourselves as instructors, we tend to treat understanding as a matter of docility and self-control: if students would just *trust us* in our expertise and *bear down* to absorb "the material," then (we think) they would be positioned to *do* the things that seem to us (in our expertise) so easy—interpreting the meaning of raw data, discerning the relative importance of facts at hand, applying learnings to new situations, creating new knowledge. We may even mean well: we can spare them from having to gain understanding the hard way! The lie of "coverage" dies hard. But, however inconvenient or heartbreaking, the truth is that learners only understand what they have "dis-covered," "un-covered," for themselves.

*Understanding can be made evident.* In our exams, in the papers we assign, in the discussions we facilitate, our students are providing evidence of *something.* We all assume, or believe, or hope that that "something" is *understanding.* But when we see the counterevidence stack up, we begin to suspect that our course activities are providing some other, tangential kinds of evidence: that our learners have learned

---

5. Ibid., 41.
6. Ibid., 44.

to say what we (the instructor) want to hear, or have succeeded in memorization tasks, or have accomplished a minimal number of educated guesses. If the kinds of resources and activities with which I am familiar do not generate evidence of understanding that I would judge to be genuine (except as an accidental feature of the work from my few natural autodidacts), then I am doomed to the *Groundhog Day* scenario painted in the introductory chapter. But what if I can imagine performances by which a student could provide compelling evidence (to anticipate the Six Facets described below) of explanation, interpretation, application, perspective, empathy, and self-knowledge?

### *"Coverage vs. Uncoverage"*

Traditional course planning begins with content. For a biblical-studies course, this "content" is often conceived in terms of selecting, say, a textbook, articles, and essays, along with a selection of biblical texts. For the traditional course planner, choosing this material is the first step in planning a course.

Let's assume that I have a set of "A" students who absorb a very high amount of content in my course, and that I have a set of "C" students who, for various reasons, struggle to absorb much content. (Playing the devil's advocate, I am assuming that these grades reflect the students' results on forced-choice, recall-based examinations.) If we were to examine both groups with a "content quiz" three months after term's end, we would find that their knowledge of content is similar. Put another way (and as is shown by studies), even students who are accomplished at memorizing and recalling information will have forgotten over 90 percent of a course's content shortly after completing the course.

At this point, the important difference is not that between those who learned the content well and those who learned it poorly. What matters is that some of these learners are motivated to revisit the course materials in order to accomplish something meaningful in their lives, and some of these learners are not so motivated. The key here, then, is the motivation to make use of the learnings. Some learners will have had some experiences during the course that prompts them to take up its subject matter again, and some learners will not have had such an experience.

I like to think of this watershed event as "a perception-changing experience of the subject matter." Facilitating such a "perception-changing experience" during the course becomes (in this view) the key to having designed a learning experience with effects in the world outside the curriculum.

It is more urgent that learners make these perception-changing "dis-coveries" that "un-cover" unexpected insights by which they become better motivated and capable of *understanding* data, than that learners temporarily control data in a rote manner in response to the short-term motivations of professor approval and success in forced-choice exams.

## *"Six Facets of Understanding"*

In Stage One of UbD, we decide what *understandings* we desire for our learners. UbD acknowledges that "understanding" is not a monolith: our understanding of understanding comprises a sheaf of related (and sometimes overlapping) capabilities. For UbD, these are explanation, interpretation, application, perspective, empathy, and self-knowledge.

These facets don't substitute for Bloom's taxonomy (or revised taxonomy), and they do not have to be understood in relation to it. And, whether you conceive of Bloom's taxonomy as a hierarchy or not, you should understand that UbD's Six Facets are *not* hierarchical. This all said, readers familiar with Bloom's taxonomy may find it a fruitful "conversation partner" with which to get to know UbD's Six Facets, and may also find it helpful in Stage Two when we decide what performances our learners must accomplish as compelling evidence of having *acquired* understanding. For now, think of the "Six Facets" as describing the range of understandings that we want our learners to have acquired by the conclusion of a course, or one of that course's learning units. Here are a few ways in which students might demonstrate growth in these different facets of understanding.

1. *Explanation.* On an exam, Edward can dutifully recall the correct "identifications" for each year on the "Introduction to Hebrew Bible" timeline. But he easily confuses them in class discussion, and complains about the course being so much about "dates and places." Elisabetta interrupts, "But it makes sense when you get the story. The fall of Samaria to the Assyrians results in an explosion of writing, editing, and collecting . . . then the fall of Jerusalem to Babylon has the same effect all over again. When the Mesopotamians are busy with their own troubles, there's room for the people Israel to have a United Monarchy, or for Josiah's innovative reforms; but in between, everything revolves around dealing with the superpowers and their demands for tribute. And then many of the biblical writers will explain the whole thing in terms of Israel's faithfulness to their covenant with God— they've got their *own* story to make sense of the details."

Edward can recall (for now) that the answer to "922 BCE" is "The United Monarchy divides into two kingdoms." Elisabetta can explain why this is the correct answer, in an act of explanation that involves synthesis, analysis, and even creativity.

2. *Interpretation.* This is a facet guaranteed to bring the biblical scholars to their feet. In September, Isolde inquires after "the" meaning of a biblical text: for her, that meaning is singular, and is located simultaneously in the mind of the author and in God's plans for her life ("Does Moses mean I should fast? When should I?"). She is anxious that some biblical stories may not be "true." By December, she experiments with the range of possible meanings that a text can support. She finds that her habitual reading of Ruth (as a kind of romance novel) lacks support in the story's details, and draws on her experience as an obedient daughter to find in Ruth's character a paradox, a woman who models faithful obedience to Naomi through acts that appear *disobedient* to her culture's sexual values. Two years later,

as a teaching assistant facilitating discussion in the same class, she is intrigued by a student's counterreading, in which Ruth's acts, however surprising and self-directed on the surface, are still suffocatingly limited and directed by the mores implicit in the novella. Years later, surveying the membership data at the church to which she is newly assigned, she says to herself, "I can *explain* this church's declining membership in terms of the local economy. But what does that decline *mean*, I wonder, to those who still attend? How many different stories do they tell themselves about the decline? What might we decide that that history means for us today?"

Isolde has learned that interpretations are stories we inherit or invent to *give meaning* to data. (Often, in biblical studies as in any corpus-oriented discipline, that "data" is likewise embedded in a story that was told to give meaning to data!) These interpretations are varying, while yet accountable in some way: intrinsically to the details of the data at hand, and extrinsically to such agreed-upon desiderata as "coherence" or "thoroughness."[7]

3. *Application.* Like most Hebrew Bible students, Alton learns early in the term that the "Sea" in Genesis 1 represents the forces of chaos and death, a characterization seen also in other ancient Near Eastern creation myths. The following year, in a preaching assignment for his second homiletics course, Alton glances at the assigned psalm and (perhaps with the assistance of a good commentary) finds there an image of the Davidic monarch holding his hand over "the Sea." Over lunch (his mind racing to brainstorm the assigned sermon), he hurries to enlighten a classmate, gushing over with his discovery that the Davidic king rules alongside the God of Israel, even appearing to participate in the separation of order from chaos. "Sure," his friend says casually. "Remember the 'Royal Theology' unit? How it includes both history and myth, and uses creation language to show the Davidic line ruling with God in eternity? There was an exam essay." Somewhat chagrined, Alton remembers feeling angry when he had "crashed and burned" on that question at the time. He presses his friend to join him in his brainstorming. Years later, as a military chaplain, he finds himself drawn to continually explore biblical texts relating to "the Sea," drawing on diverse biblical texts to help combat veterans and family members make narrative and intuitive meaning of death, illness, incapacity, and isolation.

Alton has discovered the joys of "matching knowledge to a context."[8] The *application* of knowledge to a new context will almost always involve a measure of *reinvention*. Like the prodigy who rediscovers Newton's calculus, the learner, pressed to solve a real-world problem, invents the understanding that he requires, realizing almost in hindsight that he is in fact transferring understanding from a prior context (interpretation of Genesis 1) to a novel one (Psalm 89, or pastoral care).

4. *Perspective.* In a discussion about the Priestly writer(s) of the Pentateuch, Paige remarks, "Well, of course authentic worship is to be preferred over mere ritualism."

---

7. Ibid., 91.
8. Ibid., 93.

A flurry of hands go up. Paige eventually clarifies that by "authentic," she means "spontaneous in form and occasion." An Episcopal student describes the importance that the fixed forms of the morning and evening office have for her. A Pentecostal student agrees with Paige, but good-naturedly assures her that her United Methodist services aren't nearly as spontaneous and unpredictable as she seems to assume. As things circle back around to the Priestly writer, Paige watches the instructor closely, trying to discern from his demeanor which of these perspectives is the right one.

As children, "everyone knows" that the earth is down and the sky is up. Eventually, we come to understand that this is only true from a physically limited perspective. When G. Ernest Wright wrote *The Old Testament Against Its Environment* (1950), "everybody knew" that what makes a person, group, or idea theologically significant is whatever makes it unique among others, as opposed to characteristics that it "borrows," or that "infiltrate" it. (New Testament scholars may be reminded of the "criterion of dissimilarity" in historical-Jesus conversations.) To ask *why* this must be so, why "theological significance" might not be perceived within an array of characteristics shared among many, is to recognize Wright's presupposition as embedded in a perspective. Paige has had to realize that what she saw as "just the facts" proves to be a perspective—though we leave her still trying to discern what the "right" perspective is (defined as "what the teacher thinks"). In time, when becoming acquainted with any new knowledge or claim, Paige will make a point of taking this as an opportunity to *discover* from whose perspective(s) this knowledge or claim is true, and to uncover as many differing perspectives on that knowledge or claim that she can find out. Rather than trying to wade through perspectives to grasp content, Paige will see content as an opportunity to discover perspectives.[9]

5. *Empathy.* Although Eddie is a first-term student, his Hebrew Bible/Old Testament instructor has opportunity (as his advisor) to get to know him in course-planning conversations and orientation ice-breakers. He makes friends quickly and has a good word to say about everybody. Nonetheless, the instructor find him abrupt and oddly judgmental in class: the Canaanites and the northern kingdom of Israel "got what they asked for" for disobeying God; he skips many readings, dismissing most critical biblical scholarship as racist; inadvertently, he deeply hurts a fellow student (suffering a family loss) when he opines authoritatively that "if you find God absent in your life, He's not the one who moved!" Oddly (as the instructor observes through a Facebook status update about the HBO TV series *Game of Thrones*), Eddie describes himself as enthusiastically empathetic to characters in the fantasy book series *A Song of Ice and Fire*, on which that HBO show is based. "I just love getting into the shoes of different kinds of people, in all these different situations."

Later in his degree program, Eddie has a hard time in his "clinical pastoral education" experiences. His supervisors admonish him regularly to stop "preaching at" his subjects and to listen with more empathy. Gently, the instructor invites Eddie

---

9. Cf. ibid., 97.

to try bringing his enthusiasm about *Game of Thrones* characters (in all their "different situations") to his pastoral-care subjects, to biblical literary characters, and even to the white American and Western European biblical scholars whose works he has often found toxic. "What might it have been like to process through Bethel or Dan, kissing a golden-calf throne and crying that this was the God who rescued you from slavery? What sorts of experiences and cultural inheritances inform a biblical commentary's breezy exposition on 'the light' and 'the dark'? What's it like to feel anger and grief over a loss, compounded by shame because you believe that this isn't how you're 'supposed' to feel?" Eddie later reflects, "I guess it felt *safer* to get inside the mind of a Theon Greyjoy or a Cercei Lannister, and not so safe to bring that kind of thinking to the Bible, or to people I don't trust. I want learning to be safe, I want my viewpoint and values to be the right ones, and I want the Bible to make sense. And anyway, my feelings about the Bible, race, and justice go way back before I fell in love with stories. But if I can risk empathy with fantasy characters, then I can learn to take that practice into the places where the stakes are higher."

Of empathy, Wiggins and McTighe write that it's a "deliberate act to find what is plausible, sensible, or meaningful in the ideas and actions of others, even if those ideas and actions are puzzling or off-putting." They continue, "Students have to learn how to open-mindedly embrace ideas, experiences, and texts that might seem strange, off-putting, or just difficult to access if they are to understand them, their value, and their connection to what is more familiar."[10]

If you have ever talked with learners about "the hermeneutical gap," or urged (as I have) that "reading the Bible is *always* a cross-cultural experience!" then empathy is a facet of understanding already near to your heart and ubiquitous in your experience.

6. *Self-Knowledge.* Once, as an exercise, I allowed my students to write questions throughout the semester for "Hananiah ben-Ishbaal," a thousand-year-old native of a village outside Megiddo who lived around 1150–150 BCE. (I was, of course, the author of ben-Ishbaal's replies, as the learners knew.) What was village life like? How did he worship? What did he think about the United Monarchy, or its dissolution, for that matter? In course evaluations, a student wryly observed, "I found Hananiah ben-Ishbaal a more satisfying correspondent than Dr. Lester. At least ben-Ishbaal usually gave me a straight answer!" Revealing herself to me later as the writer of that evaluation, Serena did a good-natured impersonation of me answering questions: "What drives you to ask that question?" "Do you mean 'God' the literary character, or the really-real God of your own experience, and why one instead of the other?" "Can we figure out what assumptions your question is making, and why we do or don't trust them?" Or, she finished with a hint of real exasperation, "Just *repeating the question back to the questioner!*" (A favorite teacher's trick, I know.)

Questions about questions are always *questions about ourselves*, because they are *our* questions. What do our questions—or, for that matter, ways of asking questions,

---

10. Ibid., 98–99.

our emotional reactions, our tried-and-true convictions, our likes and dislikes—say about *us*, rather than simply about the things and people we are asking about, reacting to, having convictions about, liking and disliking? This is "metacognition."[11] It's the kind of thing that animates a hundred essays on why the humanities are relevant to all other fields of inquiry—because they are fields of *human* inquiry. Often, learners come into our rooms assuming that "reflection," as in a "reflection paper," simply means "thinking about oneself" or "recording one's reactions." But properly, reflection involves inquiry about the self: *Why* do I react as I do? Why do I believe the things I believe, act the way I act, care about what I care about, think the way I think? Prying up the question with a crowbar to reveal the questioner underneath may sometimes be initially disorienting to the questioner. Still, as a facet of understanding, this avenue toward self-knowledge stands at the center of our conviction that the study of others' history and others' literature is a means of improving our understanding of ourselves.

## The Facets in Design

In Stage One, the Six Facets will help us to analyze the "understandings" that we say we want our learners to come away with. What *kinds* of understandings are they? Are they all in a similar vein, or do they represent a *variety* of kinds of understandings that does justice to the scope of our subject matter and to the scope of human inquiry into that content?

Similarly, in Stage Two, the Six Facets will help us generate performances that reflect a real range of understandings. For example, we may ask that our learners *explain* how Amos's social/historical context relates to his message concerning worship and economic justice. We might ask how Amos's denunciation of the "cows of Bashan" might be *interpreted* in a manner that rejects misogynistic caricatures. Learners may be asked to *apply* their knowledge about Amos's perspective to the Supreme Court's ruling in *Citizens United v. FEC*. And so on.

## "Big Ideas and Essential Questions"

 Much of this section appeared, in earlier form, in a blog post at Seminariumblog.org, entitled, "Hey, Instructors: Show Us Your Essential Questions!"[12]

Understanding by Design seeks to avoid the "twin sins" of traditional design: activity-oriented design, and coverage-oriented design. Instead, UbD teaches toward "enduring understanding." These are articulated in terms of essential questions

---

11. Ibid., 101.
12. QR code URL: http://seminariumblog.org/curator/lesterb92013/.

that reflect a manageable set of "big ideas" about the subject matter. Some quick definitions:

1. Big Ideas: "The core concepts, principles, theories, and processes that should serve as the focal point of curricula, instruction, and assessment."[13] These should be important, enduring, and "transferable beyond the scope of a particular unit."

2. Essential Question: "A question that lies at the heart of a subject or curriculum . . . and promotes inquiry or uncoverage of a subject."[14] A question "about which thoughtful and knowledgeable people may disagree."

3. Overarching Essential Question: An essential question that is not unit-specific.

4. Topical Essential Question: An essential question that is unit-specific.

5. Nonessential Question: A question that has one correct answer (a leading question), or a trivial question.

## *Four Connotations and Six Criteria*

What do we mean when we say a question is "essential"? Wiggins and McTighe suggest that there are four connotations implicit in the notion of "essential questions":

1. Essential questions are "important questions that recur throughout all our lives."[15] I have heard it said that one mark of a "great book" is that it repays rereading at every stage of one's life: *Huckleberry Finn* isn't the same book in my forties as it was in my teens, because I respond differently to the questions the book raises. Protagonist Juan Rico in Robert A. Heinlein's *Starship Troopers* is forced to ask himself anew, at every stage in his growth as a volunteer soldier, "Why do I fight?" Essential questions recur throughout our lives, presenting themselves as new and urgent because we, with our perspectives on their subjects, have changed.

2. Essential questions involve "core ideas and inquiries within a discipline."[16] "In what way is the Hebrew Bible authoritative?" is a core question in biblical studies, not only for readers of Jewish or Christian faith, but for anyone living in a United States whose "separation of church and state" is a concept under ceaseless dispute, and whose politics and media are well populated with biblical imagery, biblical themes, and claims about the Bible. "What, if anything, determines or circumscribes a text's meaning?" "What do the two Christian 'Testaments' have to do with one another?" "What can, or can't, we learn from ancient 'parallels' to biblical texts?" The question of "core ideas"

---

13. Wiggins and McTighe, *Understanding by Design*, 338.
14. Ibid., 342.
15. Ibid., 108.
16. Ibid., 109.

is more problematic in biblical studies today than before the postmodern challenge to modernism's ways of asking questions. For an obvious example, it can no longer be said that historical-critical methods are a "core" against which questions concerning the social context of the reader are "peripheral." However, the questions basic to historical criticism, about what we can know of an author's intent, and where, if anywhere, that is revealed, and how it relates to ourselves and our own local concerns, are, if anything, *more* "core" in light of the challenges brought to historical inquiry in biblical studies.

3.  Essential questions help learners "effectively inquire and make sense of important but complicated ideas, knowledge, and know-how" concerning core content.[17] Closely tied to the subject matter of a learning unit or a course, these can appear to devolve into nonessential questions. As Wiggins and McTighe make clear, few questions are *inherently* "essential"; it all depends on what is communicated to the learner about how they are invited to answer. Even an overarching-seeming question like "What is the good life?" can be, in practice, nonessential if the instructor is willing to accept only a predetermined answer in reply. At the same time, a question like "How is the book of Ruth a novella?" can be essential, if so framed as to invite open-ended exploration into the book's features and the nature of genre as a way of understanding the intentions and effects of a literary work.

4.  Essential questions are those that will "most engage a specific and diverse set of learners."[18] While UbD does not offer a program as such for constructing a "learner profile," this connotation shows the importance of constructing such a profile. The questions that engage another group of students may not engage mine! I like to introduce my learners to René Magritte's well-known painting, *Ceci n'est pas une pipe*. After some discussion on the difference between "a pipe" and "a representation of a pipe," we turn to Genesis 12–26, and I ask, "Est-ce un 'Abraham'?" My own seminary students, most of whom have been raised in the churches, find this extremely provocative; a very few have even walked out. But my friend who teaches undergraduate students tells me that many or most of them have not heard of Abraham. The question "Est-ce un 'Abraham'?" is not likely to grab them in the same way.

### Candidate Big Ideas and Essential Questions for Biblical Studies

## Big Ideas (or, Enduring Understandings)

These are some of the "big ideas" that I have found to span my course as a whole.

*   Reading the Bible is always a cross-cultural experience.

---

17. Ibid.
18. Ibid.

- Academic biblical studies is different from confessional "Bible study."
- The Bible is a library of composite texts that are substantively diverse in their understandings of God and of the world.
- Reading for "the gist" tends to produce superficial readings that reinforce our existing presuppositions about the text. Close, active reading for detail tends to produce surprising readings that challenge our existing presuppositions about the text.
- The "world behind the text" differs substantively from the "world in the text."[19]
- Texts not only reflect the worldviews in which they are produced, but also seek (through their rhetorical devices) to reproduce those worldviews in the reader.

## Overarching Essential Questions

For Wiggins and McTighe, these are questions that span all the units of a course. I also try to think of "overarching" as meaning, "having relevance outside this course altogether; relating to human experience broadly." In Jane Webster's chapter (below, ch. 5), you'll see that she describes these as "meta-questions."

- How do you make the most of a cross-cultural experience?
- What makes a "good reader"? What does it mean to "read well"?
- Can you "see" your own worldview? How or how not?
- What do we mean when we say a text/utterance "means" something?
- What makes a text/utterance "true"?
- In what ways might one consider biblical texts to be "authoritative" for oneself? In what ways might one not?
- Does the universe tend toward justice?
- Does a text/utterance mean the same thing to anyone, anywhere, at any time? How or now not?

## Topical Essential Questions

These are essential questions that are unit-specific, designed to provoke discussion and reflection in such course units as (for example) "Pentateuch," "Psalms," "Ancient Near Eastern Backgrounds," "Genre and Interpretation," or what have you. In practice, the boundary between "overarching" and "topical" essential questions is often

---

19. The substance of this understanding is common to introductory texts in Old Testament, but this particular formulation is Terry Fretheim's: see Terence E. Fretheim, Gene M. Tucker, and Charles B. Cousar, *The Pentateuch*, Interpreting Biblical Texts (Nashville: Abingdon, 1996), 22–36.

going to be fuzzy, especially as discrete units try to reinforce course-encompassing questions.

- What does it mean for speech to be "prophetic"?

- What makes a creation story "true"?

- What is "faith"? Can complaint, or charge of wrongdoing, be "faithful"?

- In what ways can biblical portraits of God in this unit be described as "diverse"? In what ways not?

- Why do Christians often minimize God's similarities to ancient Near Eastern gods (El, Baal) and maximize God's differences? Or the Israelites:Canaanites? Or Christians:Jews?

- What is "the gospel"? Is "the gospel" to be found in the Old Testament/ Hebrew Bible? How or how not?

- How does "genre" work? What does it do to you as a hearer/reader?

- What is "the good life"?

## Examples of Nonessential Questions

While the boundary between overarching and topical essential questions is often fluid, the distinction between essential and nonessential questions can be more neatly drawn: to the extent a question calls for a "right answer," it is a nonessential question (though, not necessarily a *bad* question!).

- How do the creation stories differ in their accounts? In what details do they resist harmonization?

- What activities and genres characterize "prophecy" in the ancient Near East and in the Old Testament/Hebrew Bible?

- Describe in detail the theological perspective of the Deuteronomistic History. Give examples of how its sources sometimes resist that theological perspective.

- What are the differences between "conventional" wisdom and "dissenting" wisdom in the Wisdom literature of the ancient Near East and the Old Testament/Hebrew Bible?

Again, though, *any* question, however open-ended its expression, will *function* as a nonessential question if the instructor is actually trolling for a predetermined, acceptable, "right" answer. "What is the good life?" becomes nonessential if the instructor will signal dissatisfaction to any but a fixed range of responses ("I'm holding a number behind my back."). Ask yourself: Why am I asking this question? Am I leading the students toward a fixed destination, or prompting an open-ended and unpredictable inquiry? Is the goal closure, or discovery?

## Stage Two: Determining Acceptable Evidence

Having determined where we think the learning is "going" in our course unit, we have to decide how learners will "prove" their understanding. What performances would be necessary to demonstrate understanding "beyond a reasonable doubt"?

Before describing what UbD calls "Thinking like an Assessor," I am going to offer an argument for the use of assessment rubrics that are available to one's learners and one's colleagues. But before that, I want to offer a preliminary, clarifying word on the terms *assessment* and *evaluation*.[20]

---

 In the following paragraph, I draw on the language used in this Duke University handout, "What is the difference between assessment and evaluation?"[21]

---

Many readers will already know that our assessments of student work may be "formative" or "summative." Typically, *formative assessments* do not count toward a grade in the course; we offer them to the learner as feedback, as a part of the learning process.[22] They are about the process: Is learning happening the way we hope it is? Formative assessments also have diagnostic value: they tell the instructor how well the students understand material at, say, the end of a unit, so that the instructor can make any necessary modifications to her plan for the upcoming unit(s). Formative evaluations relate to the subject matter of the course, responding to content-related student performances. *Summative evaluations* are those that count toward calculating a grade in the course. They are about the product: Does it reflect the learning expected of students? Summative evaluations may include elements distinct from course subject matter, for example, professionalism, participation, and so on.

Understanding by Design usually simply uses the word *assessment*, adding the modifier "formative" or "summative" where necessary to distinguish between the two. Here, similarly, I tend to use the word *assessment* broadly, referring both to formative assessments and, insofar as it also includes the activity of assessment, summative evaluations. I use the term *evaluation* where I specifically refer to the generation of grades.

---

20. "What is the difference between assessment and evaluation?" Duke University's Academic Resource Center, http://duke.edu/arc/documents/The%20difference%20between%20assessment%20and%20evaluation.pdf.

21. QR code URL: http://duke.edu/arc/documents/The%20difference%20between%20assessment%20and%20evaluation.pdf

22. Jane Webster and I have talked a good bit about this. She offers assignments that are "formative" in the sense of being primarily diagnostic, but which hold some weight for grading so that students can't just blow it off. I have often handled this by making such formative assignments "ungraded but mandatory": that is, if you don't do them, you don't pass. There's a conversation to pursue here, key terms including "formative assessment," "motivation," "adult learners," "agency," and others.

## Transparency in Assessment and Evaluation

Transparency in assessment is a loaded concept for faculty. Traditionally, we are not accustomed to having our discernment questioned: if it "smells like a B-plus" to us, then that is that. As transparency gains ground—for example, through the use of openly available assessment rubrics—some tension can build up around the loss of faculty privilege associated with this cultural shift. Occasionally, the lubricating norm of collegiality notwithstanding, this tension around transparency and privilege is pushed uncomfortably to the surface in some small, seismic event.

It was faculty training day for the new Learning Management System, and the vendor representative was teaching instructors to use the "grade book" function. Several faculty members protested that the software required them to enter numerical evaluations for student assignments. "But how do I simply put in a B-plus for an assignment? I don't use numbers!" The vendor addressed one of the complainants: "Look, let's say that you assign a student an 'A' on a paper that is 20 percent of their grade, a 'B-minus,' a 'B-plus,' and a 'C' on three quizzes that total 50 percent of their grade, and an A-minus on a final paper that is 30 percent of their grade. How will you combine those letter grades into that student's final grade?"

"Intuitively," admitted the instructor.[23]

This subsection is aimed at readers who harbor doubts about using assessment rubrics, or about making rubrics available to learners before they undertake their assignments. These reservations may include some uncertainty about sharing one's assessment rubrics and practices with colleagues or employers. Readers already comfortable with using rubrics available to learners and peers might skip this section—or read along to cheer from the balcony.

Understanding by Design is oriented toward K–12 learning environments, where accountability in assessments and evaluations is largely a "done deal." Particularly in public schools, standards are handed down to teachers from on high, and a large part of one's time is devoted to keeping up on assessments and evaluations generated by a process transparent to one's supervisors. In higher education generally, and in private higher ed especially, instructors tend to enjoy greater autonomy. Federal and state standards of accountability in grading exist, particularly for public colleges and universities, but also for the private schools, including stand-alone seminaries. Schools are also accountable to their accrediting agencies, who will want to see that institutional claims about assessment practices will match what is actually found in professor feedback and in the grade books. Nonetheless, in practice, the instructor in higher education—particularly the tenured professor, and particularly at the private institution—remains, in the grading process, largely master of her own domain.

---

23. In the words of Mark Twain, from *The Adventures of Tom Sawyer*, "Let us draw the curtain of charity over the remainder of this scene."

It's May as I revise this, and my Twitter feed is alive with instructors keeping one another's spirits up through the grading process, like geese in a vee-formation honking one another forward through the semester's twilight hours. Rick @NetCulture calls Twitter the "Collegiate Grading Support Network."[24]

Perhaps it seems paradoxical, then, that grading proves to be the third rail of higher education. We enjoy complaining about the burdensome nature of the process. But all the noise about "grading hell" sometimes masks a conspicuous silence about process. Knowledge is power, and (so the fear goes) the more a learner knows about how the grade is made, the more leverage they have to "grade grub" for a boost. When you're afraid, the instinct is to *cover up*. Better (so the fear says) to simply proclaim from the autonomy implicit in our expertise, "It feels to me more like a B-minus than a B." I would like to challenge this fear-based thinking, arguing that transparency is the stronger, even safer, choice.

I teach Old Testament/Hebrew Bible, largely to first-term seminarians. This means that my introductory course is a "gate-keeping course": I fail more students than do those instructors whose courses include mine as a prerequisite. (Put more simply: many of my colleagues only see the students who first pass my course.) Most of my students are, obviously, persons of religious faith; a substantive minority have ideological objections to the course material, and many others have at least an emotional adjustment to make in response to the course. Furthermore, my first eight years or so of "Intro" semesters I taught as an adjunct instructor, without even the protections of a long-term contract, to say nothing of tenure. (About three-fourths of instructional positions in higher education are non-tenure-track; about half of instructors are part-time employees.)[25] This is all to say, "Old Testament/Hebrew Bible" is a controversial course, prone to make many learners dissatisfied, and taught by an increasingly vulnerable teaching staff of at-will employees.

During my "adjunct years," transparency was my best friend. At some time during almost every year, a student (with or without having first spoken with me) would protest their grade to the office of the academic dean. This would sometimes include a self-justifying admonition that the school shouldn't be entrusting adjunct faculty with required courses. On such occasions, it was for me a matter of, if not life and death, at least potentially employment or unemployment, that I could demonstrate (1) that the student's evaluation was calculated from numbers rather than from whim, and (2) that the rubrics for such calculations were available to the student while she or he was undertaking the work. If I were to have said,

24. QR code URL: https://twitter.com/netculture/status/465641698874642433.
25. American Association of University Professors, "Background Facts on Contingent Faculty," http://www.aaup.org/issues/contingency/background-facts.

in that situation, that I calculated final grades "intuitively," I would probably (and justifiably) have ceased to be invited to teach courses at that school.

So, for the "contingent" instructor, transparency in assessments and evaluations is a life preserver, a DIY defense attorney. But what about the shrinking but persistent set of faculty members protected by tenure? I would put it briefly but (I admit) astringently: in biblical studies, in religious studies, or even the humanities generally, it is rare these days to find a teacher who does not instruct her learners that in this postmodern age, we know that "objectivity" is a chimera and that no person can stand outside herself and perceive her own biases. I encourage that instructor to write those words on an index card and affix it to the ceiling of her office, so that she will see them the next time she strokes her chin over a grade book and peers abstractly to the heavens to generate a student's final grade "intuitively."

Our goal, then, will be assessment rubrics that learners can relate overtly to the learning goals reflected in the course's or unit's big ideas and essential questions, and which communicate to the learner those standards according to which the instructor will generate formative feedback or summative evaluations.

### The Counterintuitive Feel of Stage Two in UbD

For many of us with the kind of teaching experience I have described in the introductory chapter, Stage Two is the most counterintuitive aspect of UbD. Normally, we decide on the resources and activities that make up the course—perhaps, at best, in light of desired outcomes of the kind we formulated in Stage One of UbD, but more likely on the basis of what we've tried in the past and what we've heard to work well for others in our field. Only then, in our usual practice, do we create grading standards for those activities. In UbD, however, we think like a judge and jury. If we think of genuine understanding as a "crime" in which we want to "catch" our learners, then what sorts of evidence would be required for a "conviction"? "Think of students as juries think of the accused: innocent (of understanding, skill, and so on) until proven guilty by a preponderance of evidence that is more than circumstantial. In a world of standards-based accountability, such an approach is vital."[26]

Only after we have decided what *sorts* of evidence (in the form of student performances) would "convict" a learner of understanding can we begin to decide how best to prepare the learner for such performances with an appropriate groundwork of resources and knowledge- and skill-building activities.

### Preparing for Stage Two

In the vignette that opened chapter 1, the reader could see my habitual thinking as an "activity designer," rather than as an assessor in a UbD frame of mind. What (I would ask) would my students find interesting and relevant to their concerns? ("Something with Martin Luther King Jr.!" "Something they can plug into a

---

26. Wiggins and McTighe, *Understanding by Design*, 148.

sermon!")? What will break up my own monotony in this iteration of the course? ("How about if they edit Wikipedia entries? I thought it was cool when so-and-so did that!") Given the content assigned, how shall I test them? ("That's a lot of multiple choice. Let's get some matching and short answer in there. No more long essays, though, until I get a teaching assistant again!") This kind of thinking can produce enjoyable and provocative activities, but is statistically unlikely, by itself, to produce compelling evidence of genuine understanding.

*Three basic questions* help the instructor to "think like an assessor" in a UbD mode, rather than like an "activity designer."[27] (1) "What kinds of evidence do we need" to find evidence that our learning goals are met? Thinking of the Six Facets, we can anticipate that this will include opportunities to explain, interpret, apply, offer perspective, show empathy, and demonstrate self-knowledge, all concerning the big ideas and essential questions animating the course and its units. (2) "What specific characteristics in student responses, products, or performances should we examine" in deciding how well the learner understands? This kind of reflection will help us formulate our rubrics, where each element of an assignment will be described in terms of performances that are "More than Good Enough," "Good Enough," or "Not Good Enough" (or Excellent, Adequate, and Developing, or similar). (3) "Does the proposed evidence enable us to infer a student's knowledge, skill, or understanding?" In practice, it will require multiple iterations of a course to fine-tune our work in Stage Two. Whenever learners produce evidence that is ambiguous, or that fails to align with our goals,[28] we will "tweak" our work in this stage to produce more efficient and unambiguous evidence.

When imagining how students might produce appropriate evidence of understanding, it can be helpful to distinguish between "exercises" and "problems," or between "forced-choice" and "authentic" performances.[29] In "exercises," a learner is presented with a simple task, with explicit prompts concerning the kind of approaches the learner is expected to recall and "plug in" toward finding a solution; there is one right answer, or a narrow range of right answers. The exercise can be simple (multiple choice, matching, short answer) or complex (essay, role-play, debate), but in any case involves explicit prompts toward the forced choice of a predetermined right response.

There is nothing particularly wrong or bad about forced-choice exercises, but they are sharply limited in their ability to provide evidence of understanding. Let's say that I offer a midterm exam that includes timelines, maps, multiple choice, matching, short answer, and essays that are designed to elicit particular "talking points" on critical issues (for example, on JEDP, or on conventional versus speculative Wisdom literature). In some cases, the results will tell me something about a learner's ability to translate genuine understanding into correct answers to direct prompts. In other cases, the same results may tell me only that a learner has achieved accurate recall of memorized responses, regardless of fuller understanding. Poor results may, in some cases, represent a learner's unfamiliarity with

27. Ibid., 150–51.
28. Ibid., 150.
29. Ibid., 153–57.

the formats of a forced-choice exam, even if her understanding is at a fairly high level. Forced-choice exercises, even of varying kinds, can serve as part of a two-way diagnostic (regarding how well learners are learning and how well the course is teaching), but will need to be supplemented by a substantive set of authentic, problem-based performance tasks.

In a genuine "problem" or "authentic" performance, the task at hand is clear but not simple. The learner's options are veritably open-ended, without prompts guiding her to a "correct" approach. The problem is described in an intentionally "noisy" and off-balance way, mirroring real-life problems where not every piece of the picture has a "purpose" toward generation of a solution. When I assign a true "problem," assessment is far more about the *features* of the learner's work than about the "rightness" of their solution. I may be completely blindsided by the solution a learner finds to a problem, but that doesn't make it wrong. I'll be asking questions like, "Does the work incorporate the materials and methods of the course unit in a substantive way?" "Does this solution generate evidence of understanding according to the performance rubrics accompanying the assignment?"

### Deriving Stage Two from Stage One

The basic formula is to say, "*If* the desired result is for learners to understand that (big ideas here) and thoughtfully consider (essential questions here), then you need evidence of the student's ability to (embodiments of Six Facets of Understanding here). So the assessments need to require something like (candidate performance tasks here)."[30]

So, for example, let's say that I draw from my list of big ideas and essential questions, deciding that I wish for learners to understand that the "history behind the text" differs substantively from the "history in the text," and that I wish them to consider thoughtfully such questions as "What is meant by a 'hermeneutic of suspicion'? and "What do we mean when we say that a story is 'true' or has 'truth'?"

Drawing on the Six Facets of Understanding, I may say that learners will need to *explain* how ancient and modern authors understood the writing of history and its purposes; what the phrase "hermeneutic of suspicion" means in the discipline of biblical studies; what kinds of "truth" we normally associate with narratives and other relevant genres of literature. They will need to *interpret* one or more biblical narratives, showing that the text is not self-interpreting and offering "legitimate but varying" readings. The learners will have to *apply* the text in the construction of some artifact (a reflection, a sermon outline, a proposed approach to a pastoral-care case). They should *see from multiple points of view*, assessing the effects of their own or other interpretations according to the varying social contexts of real readers. Learners should *empathize with* readers who are unnerved by claims that a biblical narrative is demonstrably false historically, or who have suffered harm from traditional readings that flatly assume the historicity of biblical narratives. They will need to *reflect on their self-understanding*, asking where they have benefited

---

30. Ibid., 162.

from or been harmed by readings assuming the historicity of biblical narratives, or where their own "comfort zone" lies regarding a hermeneutic of suspicion.

So, my assessments ought to require relevant performance tasks, asking students to, say, develop a "suspicious guide" to a particular biblical text, contrasting its claims to known counterevidence concerning the period it depicts. They might discuss how the Bible is or isn't "just different" (for them) from such historical fictions as Shakespeare's *Julius Caesar*, Anita Diamont's *The Red Tent*, or Jean M. Auel's *The Clan of the Cave Bear*, or such obviously tendentious histories as pre–civil-rights-era histories of the United States. They might conduct and present research on the current state of understanding of some well-known historical narrative, such as the book of Joshua's chapters on the Israelites' entry into Canaan.

As you can see, such reflections bring us to the brink of Stage Three.

## Stage Three: Planning Learning Experiences and Instruction

It has seemed a long journey to get to the point where one is finally ready to, you know, *plan the course*. This, though, is only true if we still think of "planning the course" as "deciding on resources and activities." But we're past that thinking now. At this point, deciding on resources and activities should not take long at all. We are prepared to do so in a directed, goal-oriented way.

### *WHERETO*

Before my discovery of UbD, I had already (through my online-pedagogy program) lucked upon the concept of "learning cycles." Previously, I tended toward the ineffective learning cycle that I inherited from my forebears: teach the content, then provide opportunities to show mastery of said content. In this certification program, though, I became acquainted with a learning cycle developed by Judy Neill, one that provided better results in the classroom: Motivation, Comprehension, Practice, Application.[31]

 Go here to see Judy Neill's learning cycle.[32]

Those role models in my life to whom I looked for guidance already, I realized, embodied the principles behind this approach to a learning cycle: they would first elicit their learners' attention and interest, provoking them to want to inquire into the subject at hand. They would then offer such content as answered that interest.

31. http://learningdesignresources.wikispaces.com/file/view/PracticeMakesLearning.
32. QR code URL: http://learningdesignresources.wikispaces.com/file/view/PracticeMakesLearning
.pdf/30695139/PracticeMakesLearning.pdf

Learners would have opportunity to practice their knowledge and skill, perhaps on forced-choice exercises with explicit prompts concerning how to draw on their developing knowledge and skills toward a right answer. Finally, learners would be invited to apply their understanding to real-world problems.

In UbD, this kind of learning cycle is embedded in the acronym "WHERETO":[33]

- WHERE is the work going, and why is it going there? What criteria will be employed in assessment?

- HOOK, or motivate, the learner, and HOLD their attention.

- EQUIP the learners with such resources and activities as will prepare them to meet the planned performance goals.

- Give learners periodic opportunities to RETHINK the course's "big ideas," to REFLECT on their progress, and to REVISE their work.

- Create opportunities for learners to EVALUATE their progress and self-assess (think of "assessment" broadly, including formal and informal formative assessments).

- TAILOR the course and its units to "reflect individual talents, interests, styles, and needs." (This suggests, and should aid, repeated iterations on one's "learner profile.")

- ORGANIZE the course and its units toward deep understanding (discovery, un-covering), rather than "superficial coverage."

## GRASPS

Many of us will have more experience creating forced-choice exercises than we have with authentic problems, especially with problems geared toward eliciting convincing evidence of understanding as in UbD. A helpful tool for generating such authentic performance tasks is "GRASPS."[34] I will offer examples of using GRASPS in biblical-studies assignments in the next chapter, but briefly, the design is this (the audience for these prompts is the learner):

*Goal*: You have a task, a goal, a challenge to overcome with certain obstacles. For example, you need to create an adult-education series for a group of congregants who are planning a two-week trip to the Holy Land. Your challenge is to motivate them to achieve understanding about the history and geography relevant to major sites they are likely to visit.

*Role*: You are new to the congregation and serving as associate pastor. Congregants are known to have warned one another that you are "fresh out of seminary" and likely to be bursting with "academic" data largely irrelevant to a life of faith.

---

33. Wiggins and McTighe, *Understanding by Design*, 197–98, 354.
34. Ibid., 157–60.

*Audience*: The adult-ed group is usually a small, self-selected group of curious and open-minded autodidacts. However, *your audience* is the Holy Land group, which is more representative of the congregation as a whole, including many who never come to adult-ed series.

*Situation*: The context is an affluent suburban congregation, eager for personally fulfilling experiences while pleased to dedicate themselves to regular, if perfunctory, service activities.

*Product, Performance, and Purpose*: You will create a plan for a four-week program of sixty-minute sessions, taking place weekly on Wednesday nights in place of the usual Bible study, *in order to* prepare the tour group to inquire meaningfully into the significance(s) of the sites they will visit on their Holy Land tour, *so that* the congregation will be challenged substantively concerning the "otherness" or "strangeness" of the biblical world, and especially the lack of "Jesus" in the context of such Old Testament sites as Megiddo or Hebron.

*Standards and Criteria for Success: Your performance needs to create an hour-by-hour plan for each of the four sessions, along with an accompanying statement describing the purpose of each planned element. Your work will be judged according to the accompanying rubric, meeting the standards stated therein.*

### Putting the Rubber to the Road

In the next chapter, I will offer examples (past and present) of developing actual course units in biblical studies using UbD.

## Works Cited

American Association of University Professors. "Background Facts on Contingent Faculty," http://www.aaup.org/issues/contingency/background-facts.

Duke University's Academic Resource Center. "What is the difference between assessment and evaluation?" http://duke.edu/arc/documents/The%20difference%20between%20 assessment%20and%20evaluation.pdf.

Fretheim, Terence E., Gene M. Tucker, and Charles B. Cousar. *The Pentateuch*. Interpreting Biblical Texts. Nashville: Abingdon, 1996.

Lester, G. Brooke. "Hey, Instructors! Show Us Your Essential Questions." http://seminarium-blog.org/curator/lesterb92013/.

Neill, Judy. "Practice Makes Learning." http://learningdesignresources.wikispaces.com/file/view/PracticeMakesLearning.pdf.

Rick@netculture. https://twitter.com/netculture/status/465641698874642433.

Wiggins, Grant P., and Jay McTighe. *Understanding by Design Professional Development Workbook*. Alexandria, VA: Association for Supervision and Curriculum Development, 2004.

———. *Understanding by Design*. Exp. 2nd ed. Alexandria, VA: Association for Supervision and Curriculum Development, 2005.

## Chapter 3

# Understanding by Design: Old Testament in Seminary

**G. Brooke Lester**

**A** favorite mind-game that I like to play on my students (what, you don't?) is to tell them that there is one Forbidden Question in my classes: "But Prof, how does this preach?" The "this" is some new learning or other (JEDP, 722 BCE, ideological criticism, suzerainty treaty). The motivation for the question varies; sometimes, for example, it implies, "This seems irrelevant to me, why should I have to learn it?"; other times, it implies, "I am so lost, can we distill this down to something I can grasp?" Of course, the reason I "forbid" the question is precisely in order to raise it, and the reason I raise it is to generate further questions (not, naturally, to answer the question; why on earth would I disgrace a genuine question with a straight answer?). Among the questions that arise from forbidding "How does this preach?" is the question of *context*: "Why do you assume that 'How does this preach' has one answer? Why should the text say the same thing to all hearers, in all circumstances, as interpreted by all speakers?" Something only means what it means in a *context*.

Just as preaching represents the intersection of a particular proclaimer, particular hearers, and particular circumstances, so it is with teaching and learning. In order to uncover some ideal uses of UbD, you'll want to consider (1) where the learning is happening, (2) who is learning, and (3) who is facilitating the learning. Jane Webster and Christopher Jones, the other two contributors to this volume, each begin the story of their journey with UbD by describing their context. Here, I emulate their example, describing my teaching environment, my learners, and what I bring to the process as an educator.

---

*http://seminariumblog.org/curator/

**33**

## The School

Outside my office window is Dearborn Telescope Observatory, one of the last working astronomical telescopes using a traditional glass lens. On Friday evenings, it's open to visitors, and graduate students offer demonstrations and answer questions. To me, it serves as a visual icon for a spirit of inquiry, a love of exploration. My own institution's mission statement speaks of our desire to form "bold leaders," and it's a phrase we use often, parsing out what we mean by it, individually and collectively. Working at my hipster standing desk, looking over the top of my laptop screen at the Dearborn Observatory, I allow "bold leaders" to assume synonymy with "fearless researchers" and "intrepid explorers."

My teaching context is a midsized, stand-alone seminary, Garrett-Evangelical, associated with the United Methodist Church (UMC) and sitting amidst the campus of Northwestern University in Evanston, Illinois. Our degree programs are at the master's and PhD level, though only a minority of students enter with substantive undergraduate background in religious studies. By "midsized," I mean we have about four hundred students, of whom around three-quarters are enrolled full-time, the rest being part-timers, nondegree students, and special students taking only a few classes (often as part of a degree program at a non-Methodist seminary). We are "stand-alone" in the sense that we are not part of a university or college. Although we have a historic relationship with Northwestern University going back 160 years, we are not administratively affiliated. We are one of thirteen United Methodist seminaries approved as such by the UMC's General Board of Higher Education and Ministry (GBHEM).[1] At the same time, the UMC does not share in governance of the seminary. Garrett-Evangelical is governed by a board of trustees, its administration, and its faculty. Our ratio of students to faculty is 8:1, and our seminars reflect this ratio, though a popular seminar might draw twelve or more students. A large "Intro" class can expect twenty-five to thirty students, taught by an instructor and a teaching assistant.

Some readers will wonder how education and religious formation relate to one another at a seminary; others will know that the answer depends on the nature of the denomination and of its relationship to the school. At Garrett-Evangelical, there is no requirement (as at some seminaries) that students and faculty sign a "faith statement" reflecting denominational convictions.[2] As of this writing, and to my knowledge, none of the thirteen GBHEM-approved seminaries require such a statement. While there are courses that teach United Methodist doctrine and polity (naturally, for the formation of UMC pastors), there is no institutional or academic requirement that students profess or demonstrate faith in UMC doctrine or, indeed, any particular faith commitments at all. Teaching and learning biblical studies at Garrett-Evangelical is not different from teaching it at (to draw on

---

1. According to their Web list, http://www.gbhem.org/education/seminary/approved-seminaries.
2. The word *Evangelical* in our name can be confusing in this regard. These days, many schools that self-identify as "evangelical" have such faith statements, and require (to varying degrees) that student and faculty academic work reach conclusions commensurate with these statements. Our name is the result of a merger between Garrett Biblical Institute and Evangelical Theological Seminary in 1974.

my own experience) a Presbyterian seminary (PCUSA), an Episcopal seminary (ECUSA), or a Roman Catholic school for pastoral studies. It's true that most of our learners anticipate some ordained or unordained ministry within the United Methodist Church, and are encouraged to integrate their learnings into their self-understandings as people of faith and into their vocational plans (just as are our non-Methodist learners). But the subject matter itself is not different from what you would find in a secular, university course in biblical studies: a corpus-centered Venn diagram incorporating historical inquiry, literary criticism, and cultural studies. Student work is assessed, not in reference to some catechism or statement of belief, but according to its writing mechanics, critical thinking, and control of relevant material. No "faith statement" prejudges the results of faculty scholarship. Like Galileo discovering the moons of Jupiter and thereby showing that not everything in the cosmos revolves around the Earth, we make our inquiries and let the chips (or the walls of Jericho) fall where they may.

That all said, a substantive minority of learners come to our institution with a kind of culturally infused biblical literalism. Without having particularly strong convictions about it, these students—especially those lacking lifelong habits of reading nonbiblical narrative fiction—simply have a walking-around assumption that what they read in the Bible *happened*. Once introduced to historical and literary criticism (and learning that "criticism" ≠ "nit picking," but rather = "ways of asking questions"), these students tend to make a ready adjustment to academic biblical studies. We have a smaller minority of learners who are overtly scrupulous to retain various traditional dogmatic claims about the Bible about which there is social controversy, but no evidence-based controversy, even though these convictions are not encoded in UMC doctrine and polity (for example, that Moses authored the Pentateuch, or a creationist reading of Genesis 1–2). A challenge for many teachers of "Old Testament Intro" is to support learners making these kinds of adjustments, while not falling into the trap of designing the whole course around these issues, which arguably can leave the majority ill-served.

"Public Theology": this is a new initiative at Garrett-Evangelical. In the coming years, we faculty and administrators are committed to practical experimentation in bringing our conversations and practices into the public square. This will mean different things to different participants. For my part, I tend to take scientific popularizers like Carl Sagan and Neil DeGrasse Tyson as my starting point for "public scholarship." Also, since many of the pedagogues whom I find professionally compelling already have their students doing a lot of course work on the public Web, *and* since much of my country's public discourse on the Bible is misinformed or outright deceptive, I will be looking for opportunities to engage my learners in "public biblical scholarship."

## Goals, Objectives, and Outcomes

Unlike many colleges and universities, our institution has not devised common rubrics for, say, writing mechanics or critical thinking, even within a degree program or a field of study. However, we do have a minimal set of goals articulated at the institutional level in a mission statement, and also for our various degree programs. In principle, these general goals can find more concrete expression in departmental goals, and finally (from a UbD perspective) in some of the learning objectives and outcomes embedded in our Stage-One and Stage-Two course design.

Our mission statement[3] implies the following goals: that graduating learners be "skilled, bold and articulate leaders who share the transforming love of Jesus Christ," and that they be "equipped to live and proclaim the Gospel and to teach in diverse congregations and educational settings."

Our academic handbook includes goals specific to degree programs.[4] For the ministry degrees (MDiv, MA), these goals are:

1. Personal and corporate spiritual formation: growth in knowledge of God and of faith through personal formation and covenantal communities of prayer and mission so the student lives with integrity, enhances personal and emotional health (self-care), is empowered by the Gospel of Jesus Christ, and engages in prophetic interaction and evangelical witness in a diverse society.

2. Knowing, understanding, and interpreting the theological tradition: developing as a theologian in the practice of ministry with attention to capacities for critical, reflective, faithful, and creative thinking and doing in ministry.

3. Professional ministerial practice: developing as a leader and reflective practitioner in ministry, mission, and outreach.

For the research- and teaching-related degree programs (MTS, PhD), there is no corresponding list of goals. There is only a descriptive note that these degrees "provide a specialized focus in the study of the Christian tradition and its practices." Since an MTS student will take a large core set of courses in common with the "ministry-degree" students (while concentrating in a given field and writing a thesis), one can assume that our goals for MTS students include, but are not limited to, those for ministry students.

Ideally, each field (which is what we have instead of "departments") would collaborate to write field-specific goals based on these institutional and degree-specific goals. Our fields are Bible (OT and NT); Church History; Theology, Ethics, and Society; Preaching, Worship, and Church Music; Pastoral Psychology; Christian Education; and Congregational Leadership ("United Methodist Studies" functions as a de facto field as well). However, the institution's fields have not been required or encouraged to write such field-specific goals. So, I find it helpful to devise a rough-and-ready set of Bible-specific goals, as a kind of bridge toward finding course-specific goals that in some way reflect our institutional and degree-specific goals. For example, "skilled, bold, and articulate leaders" may imply:

---

3. http://www.garrett.edu/who-we-are.
4. https://mygets.garrett.edu/ICS/Academic_Offices/Office_of_the_Registrar/Academic_and_Program _Handbooks.jnz.

- *Skilled* in the field's major historical, literary, and cultural interpretive approaches;
- *Bold* researchers who follow evidence unflinchingly even where it challenges traditional or deeply felt religious doctrine or convictions;
- *Articulate* ability to express oneself in the venues and genres appropriate to the field: research papers, prepared presentations, exegesis, reflection, analysis of literature and of arguments, and so on;
- *Leadership* in terms both organizational (facilitating activities, leading teams) and ethical (challenging entrenched hierarchies, "checking privilege," advocating for unpopular perspectives).

These could be further explored in light of the degree goals. For example, "critical, reflective, faithful, and creative thinking and doing" may imply:

- *Critical thinking and doing* in such terms as expressed in Susan Wolcott and Cindy Lynch's "Steps for Better Thinking" graphic models and rubrics;[5]
- *Reflective thinking and doing* in a self-aware mode as expressed in Norman Gottwald's "Self-Inventory on Biblical Hermeneutics";[6]
- *creative thinking and doing* as an informed improvisational response to novel questions, challenges, or situations; as originality of thought; as an open-ended, exploratory seeking of connections even where the learner's control of the material is still taking shape.

---

 For Wolcott and Lynch's "Steps for Better Thinking" graphic models and rubrics, go here:[7]

 and for a summary of Norman K. Gottwald's "Framing Biblical Interpretation at New York Theological Seminary: A Student Self-Inventory on Biblical Hermeneutics," go here:[8]

---

These provisional field- or department-level goals do not limit the possibilities for course-specific or unit-specific learning outcomes. They serve as a starting place, however, grounded in the higher-level institutional goals for learners. From this starting place, I am in a position to craft learning outcomes that do not simply

---

5. http://www.wolcottlynch.com/EducatorResources.html.
6. See, for example, Clawson's description, http://julieclawson.com/2010/09/12/self-inventory -on-biblical-hermenuetics/.
7. QR code URL: http://www.radford.edu/content/dam/departments/administrative/QEP/Lesson Ideas/Critical20ThinkingActivities.pdf.
8. QR code URL: http://julieclawson.com/2010/09/12/self-inventory-on-biblical-hermenuetics/.

arise from my idiosyncratic passions, but which, rather, acknowledge and reflect the institutional context in which (after all) my learners need to make their way. Personally, I find this grounding incredibly helpful, so that I'm not just "lost in space" as I begin to undertake crafting learning goals for my course units. I'm a part in a larger machine—one with a *lot* of autonomy and freedom of movement, but toward visible outcomes.

## The Learners

Understanding by Design does not include the construction of a "learner profile" as such, but I find it helpful to keep such a profile and consult it when beginning a new design or revising a course. (Instructional designers will already be familiar with the explicit role of learner profiling in such design approaches as the ADDIE, "Dick and Carey," and Kemp's instruction-design models.) The questions used in the example following come from a worksheet I filled out while completing the Professional Certification in Online Teaching, once offered by the University of Wisconsin (Madison).

1. *Age range: How old are the students (what is their age range)?* About twenty-two to sixty. Our median age has traditionally been well above thirty, but has recently dropped to about twenty-six years.

2. *Educational backgrounds: How many years of schooling have they completed and in what academic areas?* Nearly all have completed undergraduate studies or some equivalent satisfactory to admissions. These are in all areas, since many students are "second career." This means that we cannot simply see our learners as "master's students": most have no undergraduate grounding in religious studies, and so they are learning the material at an introductory level just as if they were undergraduates. At the same time, we expect master's-level quality of work and master's-level professionalism.

3. *Culture: What are the cultural backgrounds of the students?* Students are mostly from some strongly "churched" background. Garrett-Evangelical has a reputation as a relatively liberal UMC seminary—but again, this is in comparison to other UMC seminaries. So, for example, women's leadership is largely taken for granted, though some few students are obviously underprepared by their backgrounds to accept women as instructors. Students generally speak in favor of full inclusion of GLBTQ persons in the church, but many GLBTQ students nonetheless find the seminary community less than fully hospitable. Incoming students tend to be naïve in terms of religion: they take the "folk religion" on which they were raised for granted.

4. *Employment and family responsibilities: What kinds of jobs or family responsibilities might they have? Are they apt to be part-time or full-time students?* Far too many students have substantial responsibilities to a

church while enrolled, even before they begin a program of "field education" (which they undertake for two of their three years of study). Despite efforts by the admissions office and orientation leaders, many incoming students do not yet comprehend how much time their studies will demand. The average student is full-time, but *not* in a position to spend, say, at least two hours outside of class for every hour inside of class.

5. *Geographic locations: Where are the students located (are they local, within driving distance, statewide, national, international)?* Most of our students are residential, living in apartments near campus. A small number are in dormitories. A large minority are commuters or "distant" learners, the latter doing most or all of their study in online courses. (Since many or most of our residential and commuting students also take these same online courses, these "distant" students are integrated into the student body in this respect.)

6. *Computer access: Are they likely to have access to a multimedia computer to view text, graphics, audio, and video?* Yes, nearly all new students come with computers. We make potential online students aware of the minimum requirements: computer with a minimum Windows/Mac/Linux operating system, Web browser restrictions, ability to play streaming audio/video from sites such as at YouTube or Hulu, and any third-party software requirements.

7. *Internet/Web access: How likely are they to have access to the Internet/Web? Might it be high-speed access or low-speed telephone modem?* On campus, we enjoy screaming fast, wide-throttle broadband. We make apartment-dwelling, commuting, and online students aware that a residential broadband connection (DSL, cable) will likely suffice, whereas a dial-up/modem connection will not. I think we might also begin including a note that 3G/4G access (as with a cellular provider's USB "stick" or "wand," or using a cell phone as a modem) may or may not suffice. In the summers, we offer a special program for unordained local pastors. Many of these learners live in rural communities with limited access to the Internet, and only have broadband (cable or DSL) in their church buildings.

8. *Online learning experience: How likely are they to have experience with online learning?* Just a couple of years ago, I would say that very few would have such experience. As our median age drops, more incoming students have had undergraduate experience with online learning. Interestingly, a consequence of this is that they have particular and high expectations about consistency and quality in online learning.

9. *Learning needs: What might these students want or need to learn in terms of knowledge, skills, or attitudes? What is their level of prior knowledge?* Broadly, most see the degree as a professional degree rather than

academic, with a sizable minority enthusiastic about open-ended learning. They have church experience, and often expect to be able to have a front-ended "guarantee" that course content will have a specified, direct application in ministry (usually meaning preaching and pastoral care). Prior knowledge runs the spectrum, with many second-career students from all walks.

10. *Motivations: What goals, motivations, or reasons do they have for enrolling in your course?* See #9. For some, the degree is simply a necessary hurdle for ministry. Others are excited for the material, though many will share some misgivings about an "academic" approach to the Bible, and about the Hebrew Bible (Old Testament) especially.

11. *Language skills: What is their likely skill level in English reading and writing?* A sizable minority are English-language learners, usually Korean. Of the English-dominant students, only a minority have developed writing skills in their undergraduate work. Most have not done independent research or constructed a proper argument, and will write their first thesis papers in my course.

12. *Computer skills: What is their likely skill level in using computers? What skills do I want them to develop during the course?* Each year, skill levels are higher. Most seem confident and accomplish things like establishing user names and passwords, or downloading third-party software to play specialized audio/video content. A small minority are almost helpless. I want them to control their word processor and follow typographic instructions; to control the Learning Management System (LMS); and to be able to do some work on the Web, usually with pseudonymous user names. I often ask them to do some minimal social networking (Twitter, social bookmarking). Increasingly, I require learners to undertake such multimedia projects as a voice-recorded presentation or an audio-visual book trailer.

13. *Learning skills: What is their likely level of cognitive and metacognitive skills in knowing how to learn and to manage the learning process? What skills do I want them to develop during the course?* This is quite low in general, except the few with a degree in education. What is worse, many of them have a layperson's acquaintance with the Myers-Briggs Type Indicator, multiple intelligences, or other scalar measuring tools: just enough for them to declare with high confidence and low accuracy what they can/will and what they can't/won't attempt in our course work. I want them to identify themselves as having ideological commitments out of which they read texts; to recognize their worldview as historically conditioned; to recognize and accomplish critical thinking about our course material. By term's end, they are to construct an argument defending an evidence-based thesis concerning a biblical text.

14. *Disabilities: What kinds of physical or learning disabilities, such as hearing or visual impairments, might students have?* We have relatively few students with physical disability. Several students self-identify to the dean of students as having some learning disability, on the basis of which they come to written agreement with their instructors about accommodation.

15. *Overall impacts: Considering the above, how diverse or homogeneous are the students? Is there a "typical student"? In what ways are the learner characteristics most apt to affect course planning and teaching?* There is no "typical student" in terms of an entire profile, but clear majorities can be established along several indicators: nearly all are confessing Christians seeking leadership in the Protestant church; most are underprepared to research and write; most are distracted by doing more church work (or other paid employment) than they should while in a full-time degree program; most do have reasonable facility with computers and the Internet, while not being serious social networkers except for Facebook. *These characteristics affect course planning and teaching thusly:* Hmmm. . . . It's fair to say that we are forced to spend considerable course time on "Composition 101" and "Critical Thinking 101"; and large, complex assignments must be broken into staged, mandatory tasks.

A "learner profile" is always a moving target, and often offers an oblique window into aspects of institutional culture. If learners are getting younger, how are faculty responding to that (and how are they responding to their disagreements about responding to that)? What faculty alliances or divisions might emerge where introductory courses have a de facto requirement to undertake remediation in addition to their regular subject matter, or otherwise serve as "gatekeeper courses," such that some other instructors may have only limited knowledge of students who are dismissed or drop out during their first year? What misunderstandings among students, faculty, and administrators might develop as a higher percentage of learners forge their communities of inquiry online, largely invisible from the standpoint of the physical plant?

## The Instructor

It looked for a minute there as if we were ready to start in on some Stage-One activity for my biblical-studies courses, didn't it? But of course, I am not the Instructor from Nowhere. What *about* those "idiosyncratic passions" with which I approach the teaching of biblical studies? What about my own background and assumptions as a pedagogue? Like you, I'm a squirming bag of experiences, opinions, resentments, accomplishments, mentors, points of gratitude, mistakes, lessons, fears, and hopes. I have a *trajectory*. It's worth holding back a moment to take this, at least briefly, into explicit account.

I earned my doctorate in Old Testament at Princeton Theological Seminary (PTS), at a time when the program boasted a large faculty and large cohorts of PhD students. Although the program included literary approaches and hermeneutics, the "meat and potatoes" of the program were history and languages: in addition to the regular seminars and advanced work in biblical languages, an Old Testament student could acquire Ugaritic, Akkadian, Aramaic, Syriac, even Middle-Kingdom Egyptian. Every PhD student served also as a Teaching Fellow, a well-compensated position that included substantive time working independently with several "precepts" of a dozen or so master's students (mostly MDiv). Introductory Bible classes at PTS were large, often containing over one hundred students. In part for this reason, the courses had a well-defined structure that changed little over time: Teaching Fellows would refer to it as the "well-oiled machine." Although we PhD students conferred together almost constantly about our teaching and grading, these discussions revolved around *episodes*: what happened, what we had done, how we might respond differently next time. It would not have occurred to me to reflect on a course's design as such, since course revision was not (in my time) ever brought up. (Those of us lucky enough to do additional work as Teaching Fellows for advanced-level courses might have some opportunity to engage in collaborative reflection on design choices, if the instructor invited it.) For a period, a number of us joined in a project that examined inductive approaches to the teaching of biblical languages. I recall a pedagogy workshop of one or two afternoons, resulting in an appropriate acknowledgment on my transcript. In general, though, we internalized the norms typical to the formation of terminal degree holders: our primary formation is as scholars, and challenges relating to teaching the field's content are solvable on an ad hoc basis by critical imitation of one's mentors, informal commiseration with one's peers, and practice, practice, practice.

Online learning presented itself to me, in time, as an opportunity to learn something of "pedagogy" as a field in its own right. Obviously, I'm not alone in this: as institutions have sought to make sound decisions about online learning (and to justify those decisions publicly *as* sound), explicit public reflection on the nature of learning has swept higher education in a way that is, as far as I can see, unprecedented, and undeniably for the good. My own enthusiasm for the theory and practice of digital pedagogy has led directly to my current position, a full-time faculty member who coordinates his institution's practices in digital learning and seeks to model, in his courses, innovation appropriate to the school's emerging vision. I graduated with an "Old Testament" degree in 2008; if I had not found this digital-learning "niche" within my current institution, I would still be waiting tables.

As to my "idiosyncratic passions" relating to biblical studies, these include but are not limited to the following convictions:

- The best reason to learn biblical studies is self-defense. There is more nonsense uttered in the public sphere about the Bible than about any other topic (save *possibly* sex), all of which is designed to make citizens act and vote in certain ways. Like sheep among wolves, people in the United States absorb their knowledge of the Bible from charlatans, demagogues, and well-meaning fools. A rigorous program in academic biblical studies qualifies the graduate to perform as a shepherd, with all the rights pertaining thereto, to wit: bashing the heads of lions and bears.

- The best possible preparation for academic biblical studies is a lifelong habit of reading fiction and poetry for pleasure: a student will ideally already have the experience of having been *moved and changed* by fiction. A little is better than none, and it's never too late to start, but its absence is a substantive disadvantage. Possible substitutes include any other background in life that has forced one's development of *empathy*.

- Academic biblical studies is for everybody. There is no religious litmus test qualifying one to engage in biblical studies. There are no points earned for having reached conclusions orthodox to a religious tradition (nor, for that matter, for conclusions iconoclastic to any tradition). If you are picky about company, then stick with some in-house Sunday school where everyone can be counted upon to reinforce one another's presuppositions. But I recommend that you first give us a try.

- Correction to the above: academic biblical studies is for *grown-ups*.[9] Children of all ages need not apply.

The institution, with its goals. The learners and the instructor, with their respective backgrounds, presuppositions, and urgent concerns. With these firmly in view, hanging on the wall above the desk, so to speak, we are in a position to undertake an informed beginning on Stage-One activity for a pair of courses at Garrett-Evangelical: a seminar on "The Old Testament in the New Testament," and "Intro to OT" taught as a Massive, Open, Online Course (MOOC): the "Open Old Testament Learning Event."

## OT in the NT by Design

"The Old Testament in the New Testament" is a course I have taught once before, in 2010, and I am taking it up again in Fall 2014. As the title suggests, students examine all those ways in which New Testament texts refer (overtly or covertly) to older texts that are known to us in the Hebrew Bible/Old Testament. My dissertation, defended in 2007, involved allusions to Isaiah in the book of Daniel, bringing me into the confused fray of scholars who write about "inner-biblical exegesis," "inner-biblical allusion," or "intertextuality in the Bible."[10] In my continuing research and writing, I distinguish "allusion" from other forms of intertextual reference, defining it as a text-intended figurative trope.[11] The course itself has two ongoing areas of focus. The first area of focus is the biblical material itself: What are the peculiar

---

9. Hat tip to David G. Garber, associate professor of Old Testament and Hebrew at the McAfee School of Theology at Mercer University.

10. "Daniel Evokes Isaiah: The Rule of the Nations in Apocalyptic Allusion-Narrative," PhD diss., Princeton Theological Seminary, 2008.

11. If you're interested, I recommend not only Ziva Ben-Porat, "The Poetics of Literary Allusion," *PTL: A Journal for Descriptive Poetics and Theory of Literature* 1 (1976): 105–128; but also and especially Gian Biagio Conte and Charles Segal, *The Rhetoric of Imitation: Genre and Poetic Memory in Virgil and Other*

ways in which different NT authors press OT texts into rhetorical service? The second area of focus is the scholarship on "inner-biblical interpretation": What are the ongoing points of confusion, why do they persist, and whom do they serve?

The big "twist" for this iteration is the in-class student presentations, which are to be live-streamed on the Web and captured as recordings. In my seminars, I have gradually built up strategies for eliciting more professional presentations from students. The standard-issue, seminary-student presentation is a nightmare of boredom: a static summary of some part of the reading, delivered from a seated position, followed by an invitation to obligatory, undirected, unstructured discussion. Instead, I ask students to deliver their presentations in professional dress, standing, with a podium as a home base (from which they can wander at will), including a mandatory audio-visual slideshow following Mark Sample's "1/1/5 Rule": at least *one* image per slide; each slide used only *once*, and no more than *five* words per slide.[12] Students are expected to speak from notes, rather than read a text; part of our preparation is to discuss how good presenters "know their narrative," such that they could—if forced—proceed even without slides and notes.[13]

---

      Go here to read more about Mark Sample's "1/1/5 Rule."[14]

---

In this course, we up the ante a step further: we will promote our in-class presentations through Twitter and Facebook, then live-stream them to the Web and capture them as recordings. By term's end, the students will combine these presentations with select course materials and external Web links, creating an online "exhibit" introducing laypeople to the topic of "The Old Testament in the New Testament." Thus, students complete the course with an artifact that has enduring usefulness after the term's end.

Like most of us who teach an elective on a topic near our hearts, I have some selfish reasons for offering "The Old Testament in the New Testament." It is not that I get to have graduate students "do my research for me": they are only reading stuff that I have already pored over several times, including a couple of pieces that I have written. Rather, I think we both benefit, student and instructor, from those moments of genuine discovery where we find ourselves co-learners and co-discoverers. The course's methodological readings, with which I grappled during my dissertation and early-career writing, are complicated and are frustratingly prone to talk past one another. (Dealing with this aspect of scholarship is a major theme

---

*Latin Poets*, Cornell Studies in Classical Philology 44 (Ithaca: Cornell University Press, 1986); and Carmela Perri, "On Alluding," *Poetics* 7 (1978): 289–307.

12. http://chronicle.com/blogs/profhacker/challenging-the-presentation-paradigm-with-the-115-rule.

13. See the appendix, exhibit 1, below, for my rubric on grading presentations.

14. QR code URL: http://chronicle.com/blogs/profhacker/challenging-the-presentation-paradigm-with-the-115-rule.

in the course.) When I taught the course before, it would happen occasionally that a student makes some breakthrough in the methodological literature, challenging or even correcting some misunderstanding of my own. This doesn't bother me at all, as I don't find it really awkward to have to include "retractions" in my subsequent writing. After all, why publish again on a given topic if it does not continue to catch me flat-footed from time to time? (Hey, *you* read Gian Conte's *Rhetoric of Imitation* and we'll see what *you* get out of it on the first half-dozen readings.) And it's not only I who gains from such moments: these make for exciting times for the learners, especially for MDiv students who often do not think of themselves as "academics" so much as trade-school types. In any case, this is all to say that I am trying for the best of what an instructor's-pet-research-topic elective can be. Once some of the students realize that I take their readings seriously toward the solutions of problems that actually keep me up nights, things tend to really hum along.

Understanding by Design works best for designing *course units*, rather than entire courses ("This bed is too large!") or individual class sessions ("This bed is too small!"). When I taught the course in 2010, I had not broken things into units. There was a sense of movement: we started with a methodological grounding, then sustained methodological reading and reflection while progressing from the Gospels, to Paul, to the pseudo-Pauline and other non-Pauline NT literature. So, here, I need to decide on a unit-based structure before settling on a representative unit to build "UbD style." It ought to become clear that this unit-building approach has the benefit of forcing the instructor to work outward in both directions, toward session planning and toward a vision for the course as a whole.

When teaching Hebrew Bible or New Testament, we usually have to decide whether to go with a (mainly) canonical or (mainly) chronological structure. Or, we can try a more experimental, topic-based structure. I don't have a strong preference, but in this case, I find that I have good reasons to take a (more or less) canonical approach. A lot of my personal "goods" in the course revolve around the nature of figurative speech and how literary allusion functions rhetorically in a way analogous to metaphor. It takes students several weeks to absorb the methodological understandings required to participate at that level, and (as it happens) most of the best examples are clustered in the Pauline epistles. So, it's just as well to plunk through the Gospels for awhile, becoming familiar especially with Matthew's relatively prosaic, nonfigurative habits of referring to the Hebrew Bible. (There are exceptions, but for the most part, Matthew's "prophecy fulfilled" texts really demand very little of the reader; he does the interpretive work, so you don't have to!) By starting with a few weeks of methodological background, and then working through the NT essentially canonically, the students have time to "warm up" and to become familiar with a lot of nonfigurative examples of the "OT in the NT" before hitting Paul. Then the non-Pauline stuff, less creative in its use of the OT but with enough of its own variety to merit attention, provides a warming-down period, sort of like static stretches following a heavy workout. So:

- Unit One (3 weeks): Methodological Background. (How the NT material raises the question, with examples; origins and brief history of scholarship; critical issues and key terms; relevance[s] for today's interpreters.)

- Unit Two (4 weeks): The OT in the Gospels (with attention to rhetorical devices and their functions, including nonfigurative and figurative use of the OT).
- Unit Three (3 weeks): The OT in Paul (with attention, ditto, etc.)
- Unit Four (3 weeks): The OT in deutero-Pauline and other epistles, and Revelation (with attention, ditto, etc. Concluding reflections.)

Each unit, then, will need to include (1) time for reading/viewing and and discussing appropriate resources, (2) time for promoting and accomplishing the in-class presentations, and (3) time for collaboratively building the online exhibit. Since Unit Three (Paul) represents a high point toward which I imagine the course building, I will use it as my "entry point," and take it here as my exemplar.

Did you catch me? As you can see, I have *already cheated* from a UbD perspective, by setting my heart on particular activities (that is, the presentations and the exhibit) before accomplishing the Stage-One and Stage-Two preparatory design work. Fortunately, UbD anticipates this: "Rather than offering a step-by-step guide to follow . . . the book provides a conceptual framework, many entry points, a design template, various tools and methods, and an accompanying set of design standards."[15]

Here, a number of factors—the institution's express mandate to explore "public theology," my evolving efforts to promote professional-level in-class oral presentations, and my commitments around teaching digital literacy and digital citizenship—conspire to form some predesign resolutions about student activities in this course. The trick will be to hold these with a "loose but firm grip," ready to modify them or, if necessary, drop them in light of my Stage-One and Stage-Two designing.

### *The Design Stages, in Short Form*

Without further ado, let's dig in to the process itself. The formula[16] that I will keep in my head is:

### Stage One:

*"If the desired result is for learners to"* meet particular *standards* (abbreviated G for "grade standards"); have certain *understandings* (abbreviated U for "understanding"); consider given *essential questions* (abbreviated Q for "questions"); to *know* certain facts and have certain *skills* (abbreviated K and S respectively) . . .

---

15. Grant P. Wiggins and Jay McTighe, *Understanding by Design*, exp. 2d ed. (Alexandria, VA: Association for Supervision and Curriculum Development, 2005), 7.
16. Derived from *ibid.*, 149 and 162)

Stage Two:

*"Then I need evidence of the student's ability to* explain, interpret, apply, see from a point of view, empathize with, reflect on such-and-so elements of our subject matter (in other words, to demonstrate the Six Facets of Understanding) . . .

*"So the assessments need to require something like"* recalling, defining, describing, developing, predicting, analyzing, adjudicating, devising. . . . That is, fill in action verbs (with appropriate predicates, of course) that will let the learners show compelling evidence of the desired understandings. I like to start out with the verbs and verb phrases from the Six Facets of Understanding. Then, I may also draw on a list of verbs arranged by columns, grouped according to Bloom's taxonomy (or revised taxonomy). These are easily found by doing a Web search for something like "Bloom's taxonomy action verbs." There is no one-to-one correspondence between the Six Facets of Understanding and Bloom's taxonomy, but I just like to have such a "well" of verbs on hand to spark my thinking.

*"This suggests the need for specific tasks or tests* (abbreviated T) *and other evidence of desired understandings"* (abbreviated OE).

Stage Three—that is, selecting resources and activities—will be pretty obviously cued up by this point, and will follow. But I am better off staying with Stage-One and Stage-Two thinking until these are more or less complete. I am trying to avoid the temptation to fall into conventional design practice, sneaking in all my pet activities and resources at the outset, then justifying them by after-the-fact retro-designing of learning objectives and assessments.

### Stage One for "OT in the NT"

*"Meet the standards . . ."* While we don't have "standards" (G) as such, we have such institutional and degree-program goals. Some include:

- Students will gain experience as "public biblical scholars."

- Students will have opportunity to use learned knowledge and skills in leadership roles.

- Students will demonstrate critical and creative thinking and doing.

*"Understand that . . ."* These enduring understandings include those relating to the subject matter and the field of biblical studies, as well as some "meta" understandings about (for example) professionalism in presentations.

- "Meaning" can be argued to reside in the text, the author, the reader, or in some interplay among two or more of these.

- "Hermeneutics" (here, shorthand simply for practically testing the range of meanings a text might support for readers in differing contexts) as we practice with biblical texts has a long pedigree, happening extensively already in the Bible itself.

- Texts don't just "tell"; they use rhetorical devices to act more directly upon the hearer.

- Figures (e.g., metaphors) overtly prompt the hearer to join actively into the co-production of meaning with the text.

- The study of allusion/intertextuality is not limited to biblical studies, but takes place in other corpus studies (Shakespeare, Milton, classics, etc.).

- New Testament authors engage in interpretive strategies that would not pass muster in an academic biblical-studies course (which is fine, since we're not "grading" them but trying to understand them).

- Not only do all scholars of "inner-biblical interpretation" not use the same jargon as one another, they often state very different goals for their study.

- Biblical studies often lags some decades behind the secular fields of its ancillary disciplines (archaeology, history, literary criticism, cultural studies, sociology, etc.).

*"Thoughtfully consider the questions . . ."* These sometimes arise directly from the "enduring understandings" first listed (above). Some, though, spring full-grown directly from my head or from the sea. Again, my plan at this point is to write it all down; I can pick and choose more narrowly later, but I prefer to do so "from abundance."

- What does metaphor (or other figures) do in the hearer, and how does it do it?

- Can one determine "the intent of the text" (for our purposes, an alluding text)? What counts as evidence for such "intent"?

- How many meanings can an Old Testament text support? What constraints, if any, does the text itself impose on the interpreting reader?

- What checking or corrective power over a reader's biases does a "methodology" offer, if any? Is "method" a straitjacket or a lab coat? When and how?

- Who benefits from persistent unclarity of terms or method? How so? Who suffers, and how? (Consider not only scholarship, but any areas of life.)

*"Know and be able to do . . ."* This is a brainstorming pass on the Knowledge (K) and Skills (S) that the learner should be able to demonstrate, drafted in reflection on the standards (G), understandings (U), and essential questions (Q) already drafted. As you can see, this is *beginning* to evoke possibilities not only for assessment (Stage Two), but for resources and activities (Stage Three).

- Use key terms such as allusion, reference, metaphor, metonymy, synecdoche, irony, poetics, referent, vehicle, tenor, synchrony, diachrony, influence, trope, figure, exegesis, hermeneutics, marker, marked. (Not all of these will be introduced in this unit; most will have been introduced in previous units).

- Be conversant with major approaches to inner-biblical interpretation, and how these have unfolded with respect to one another and to some related currents in biblical studies.

- Identify points of disagreement and incoherence in the field of "inner-biblical interpretation."

- Discuss Paul's particular inner-biblical habits, with examples.

- Be conversant with the "Intentional Fallacy" and the "Affective Fallacy," including their scope and limits as described by Wimsatt and Beardslee.[17]

### Stage Two for "OT in the NT"

While not perhaps necessary, I find it helpful to undertake Stage Two with a systematic eye on the Six Facets of Understanding, as suggested in *Understanding by Design*.[18]

*"Then you need evidence of the student's ability to . . ."*

- *Explain*: What the phrase "the OT in the NT" refers to, briefly; figuration; why scholars disagree about method, or even the importance of method.

- *Interpret*: Two NT texts that cite/allude to the same OT text, or to two similar texts, or two texts both in a larger OT pericope. For example, Matthew and Paul on texts from Isaiah 52–53.

- *Apply*: For example, Ziva Ben-Porat's approach to each of these two NT texts. Then, apply Carmela Perri's modified approach as elucidated in class.

- *See from the points of view of*: Matthew's and Paul's audiences as theorized in a major critical commentary; make explicit reference also to the exilic audience addressed in Isaiah 52–53.

- *Empathize with*: Paul's original hearers of Romans whose concerns and presuppositions do not wholly (or perhaps even substantively) match your own.

- *Reflect on*: The ways in which an OT-citing NT text does (or does not) overtly invite the reader to co-produce meaning with the text, and how this expands (or elsewise narrows) the range of possible meanings.

*"So the assessments need to require something like . . ."*

---

17. W. K. Wimsatt Jr. and M. C. Beardsley, "The Intentional Fallacy," *The Sewanee Review* 54, (1946): 468–88. Idem, "The Affective Fallacy," *The Sewanee Review* 57, (1949): 31–55.
18. *Understanding by Design*, fig. 7.8, 162. Compare to fig. 7.2, 149.

- Showing preparation in the fundamentals (e.g., that the learner can distinguish between devotional "Bible study" and academic biblical studies; that she can distinguish between the likely meanings of a text for its original audience and possible meanings of a text for later readers in differing contexts; major events on an OT-NT historical timeline).

- Imagining a three-cornered conversation about the meaning of an OT text, the participants being its author, an NT writer citing/alluding to that OT text, and a given modern Christian interpreter.

- Elucidating a particular scholar's methodological approach to "inner-biblical interpretation" or to "allusion."

- Analyzing competing methodological approaches, making claims about the relative goods of each.

- Experimentally placing modern varying interpretations of Scripture in some kind of (dis)continuity with the inner-biblical interpretive activity found within Scripture itself.

Something I may or may not do at this stage: begin hammering the above bullets into assessment rubrics. Most often, I simply make a good start, asking myself, "What would it look like for a learner to accomplish this task excellently? What would it look like for a learner to accomplish the task poorly? What kinds of errors or misunderstandings might I expect (or have I become accustomed to finding)?" These will eventually become the first and last columns in a three-column rubric with headers reading "Exceeds Expectations," "Meets Expectations," and "Developing" (or, as I think of them in my head, "More than Good Enough," "Good Enough," and "Not Good Enough"). The likely elements of the assignment each become a row in the rubric: for example, "Comprehensiveness," "Factual Accuracy," "Engagement with Course Materials," and so forth.[19]

### Stage Three for "OT in the NT"

Finally, we are ready to, you know . . . build the course. First, what kind of activities will prepare the learners to accomplish what I'm imagining for their assessments? Some possibilities include:

- *Diagnostic pre-assessment* in the "fundamentals" of academic biblical studies, perhaps in the form of an online survey, conducted anonymously but with tabulated results available to the students for reflection and discussion.

- *Role-play*, in which learners take on the roles (say) of Hosea, Matthew, and John Wesley, engaging each other in that three-cornered conversation

---

19. An excellent and widely regarded resource for educators getting started with assessment rubrics is Dannelle D. Stevens and Antonia Levi, *Introduction to Rubrics: An Assessment Tool to Save Grading Time, Convey Effective Feedback, and Promote Student Learning* (Sterling, VA: Stylus, 2005).

concerning (in this case) the meaning of Hosea 11, "Out of Egypt I have called my son."

- *Exegetical thesis paper*, in which the learner interprets (say) Matthew 8:16-17 and Romans 15:21 with attention to their use of Isaiah 53:4 and Isaiah 52:15, respectively.

- *In-class presentations*: each week (until we run out of students), a learner presents a professional-quality presentation on a methodological article or essay relating to literary allusion or inner-biblical interpretation. This presentation includes a concrete plan for facilitating a twenty-minute class activity following the twenty-five-minute presentation.

- *Discussion* exploring the more "fraught" aspects of inner-biblical interpretation for readers of religious faith ("Multiple meanings? Isn't that relativism?" "But if the OT text meant differently in its own time, then is Matthew *wrong*?" and so on). This could involve a "fishbowl" discussion format, allowing as it does a silent outer circle able to reflect privately (with or without, say, a Twitter backchannel for voluntary note passing).

What resources will the learners need in order to undertake these activities?

- A steady diet of methodological pieces, with differing objectives and approaches to the literature (easily found, with "inner-biblical interpretation" being in the state it is). Many of these will not be about the Bible at all, but represent the study of allusion in "secular" studies (classics, Milton, etc.).

- A book that attempts some comprehensive view of the "OT in the NT," even at a relatively surface level. A good example is Steve Moyise, *The Old Testament in the New: An Introduction*, T&T Clark Approaches to Biblical Studies (London: T&T Clark, 2001).

- An essay collection entirely on inner-biblical interpretation (or even "OT in the NT" specifically). A likely, if dense, candidate is Stanley E. Porter, *Hearing the Old Testament in the New Testament*, McMaster New Testament Studies (Grand Rapids: Eerdmans, 2006).

- Possibly, some short Internet pieces relevant to the course. These could be collected by the students themselves during the term, using a social bookmarking platform like Diigo.com.

After some brainstorming on the planned activities, it's a good time to look through "GRASPS" and "WHERETO," drawing on them for inspiration to shape these emergent assignments toward their most pedagogically sound realization.

And I'm off to the races.

My next example I can treat more briefly, since the explanatory work has already happened in the "OT in the NT" example. But, this second example may be of wider interest, since it treats the basic "Introduction to the Hebrew Bible/Old Testament" course. I hope it will, at the same time, be of unique interest, since it casts that basic course into a novel environment: the Massive Open Online Course, or MOOC.

## "OOTLE15" by Design

OOTLE15 ("Open Old Testament Learning Experience 2015") is a course I have planned for Spring 2015. In terms of subject matter, this is simply "Introduction to the Hebrew Bible/Old Testament." A maximum of twenty-five regularly enrolled Garrett-Evangelical students will take the course for its usual three credits. At the same time, this course will be open (not for credit and free of charge) to all interested participants, and will take place in an open, distributed format: all learners will accomplish the course activities on their own blogs, Twitter accounts, and so forth, with a publicly available course hub facilitating interaction among those distributed platforms. While sharing in a hub of course materials, learners will receive guidance to form communities of inquiry that may persist after the end of the course; to generate their own learning outcomes; to articulate their particular "big ideas and essential questions"; and to conceive of and complete a course project that will have enduring meaning for them. I hope to see about three hundred such participants, but will be pleased with one hundred or more. I believe the course can be scaled to handle a deluge larger than my hoped-for three hundred.

If you are having a hard time imagining this, it may be helpful to name some of my influences for this course. In terms of shape, I look to such online events as the Open Online Experience (OOE15), ETMOOC, and MOOCMOOC.

Links to these online learning events can be found by going to *my Seminarium* blog post, "Scarcities 2: Online Learning Platforms."[20]

For a course such as this, I like the idea of learners having the opportunity to shape their own concerns and assignments as much as possible, which implies (from a UbD perspective) that they discern some of their own big ideas and essential questions. At the same time, UbD demands that I establish these at the outset of the design process, before learners are even involved. Does UbD not work in this case? How do you design your course from its outcomes if learners will be discerning their own outcomes as part of the course? My solution is to plan my course, including its big ideas and essential questions, while *including among these* the discernment and development of the learner's own. In other words, facilitating such self-reflection and assignment crafting will be one overt element of the course. Without anticipating (too much) what kinds of Stage-Three work this might involve, I can imagine we might (for example) create a collaborative document,

---

20. QR code URL: http://seminariumblog.org/curator/lesterb82013/.

maybe a Google Doc or a Titanpad/Etherpad, in which learners can collaborate in creating their own big ideas and essential questions.

By inviting learners to drum up some ideas about what "enduring understandings" they want to pursue in OOTLE15, we also enhance the course's realization of "uncoverage" versus "coverage," a central aspect of UbD. Students learn not only how to build their online space for making and interacting, but they are forced to reflect explicitly on *why* they do so, and *what projects* might be meaningful to them, and *what kinds of connections* they want to make with others, and with whom. These discoveries take time, which means less time on covering content; but such discoveries are necessary to being able to meaningfully approach what content *is* covered.

Provisionally, I plan for OOTLE15 to include five units: (1) Introduction to Academic Biblical Studies and to the Hebrew Bible, (2) The Writings, (3) The Latter Prophets, (4) The Former Prophets, and (5) The Pentateuch. The first unit is a good idea for any "Intro to HB/OT" class, since students are usually first-semester seminarians and often imagine that seminary courses are a kind of "church-plus." But for OOTLE15, an introductory grounding in the norms and practices of "academic biblical studies" is all the more urgent, since who even *knows* what kinds of expectations our not-for-credit participants will be coming in with. I *want* a wide variety, and plan to promote the course transparently, but it's important that registrants have a fair opportunity to realize that they're in the wrong room, so to speak, if our agenda is not what they're looking for.

And, yes, you read rightly: I take the Hebrew Bible backward, beginning with the Writings and concluding with the Pentateuch. This has *nothing* to do with "backward course design" in a UbD sense. Rather, it's something I began after complaining to a teaching assistant after class (for the hundredth time), "They could read the Pentateuch and the Former Prophets *so much better* if they only had already had the Writings! They don't know yet that the HB/OT embraces competing theologies and happily charges God with wrongdoing. Also, could the Documentary Hypothesis *possibly* involve more dates and geography? Shoot me now." Starting with the Writings, they get the above-ranted important big ideas right off the bat, and only need dates from the destruction of Jerusalem (587/586) forward. This raises questions about how the exile came to pass, so then they're primed for the Latter Prophets (taking us back to the years preceding 722 and the fall of Samaria)—while learning that the Prophets, like the Writings, have gripes and exhortations wildly different from one another. Questions about the fall of Samaria lead naturally to the Former Prophets, bringing us back to emergence of Israel in the land and the premonarchical period. So, when we finally get to the Pentateuch, not only do they have a sporting chance to make sense of the Documentary Hypothesis, but attempt it armed with a by-now-solid understanding of "academic biblical studies" and a clearheaded sense that they *don't* know what they'll find there—since, as the study of the rest of the HB/OT has hopefully shown, the reader might find almost *anything* in there.[21]

---

21. "Full Reverse! The OT/HB from Writings to Torah," http://seminariumblog.org/curator /lesterb32013/.

I have blogged about "Learning the Hebrew Bible Backward" at *Seminarium*, and as a link there shows, previously at my personal site.[22]

Here, I begin design with the second unit, "Writings." After all, this is the unit that inspired my current "backward-through-the-Hebrew-Bible" approach. I expect that the brainstorming I do here will yield concepts that really belong in the introductory unit; but, as when planning "OT in the NT," I'd rather get it all down on paper now, and only later edit from that abundance.

### Stage One for "OOTLE15"

*"Meet the standards . . ."* Again drawing on institutional and degree-program goals to serve as top-level "standards" (G), these may include:

- Students will gain experience as "public biblical scholars."
- Students will have opportunity to use learned knowledge and skills in leadership roles.
- Students will encounter diverse understandings of the Hebrew Bible.

*"Understand that . . ."*

- Academic biblical studies is not the same as devotional Bible study, with regard to the "3 P's": presuppositions, participants, and procedures.
- Reading the Writings (and the HB/OT generally) is always a *cross-cultural experience*.
- The Writings are *diverse* in their understandings and claims about God and the world.
- Reading complicated works (like Job) for the "gist" or "message" tends to produce facile, bias-confirming interpretations.
- Attribution of biblical books and collections to venerable ancient figures from the past (Samuel, David, Solomon, Daniel) begins late in the biblical period and largely postdates the substance of such works.
- Texts not only *reflect* the worldviews in which the texts take shape, but seek through their rhetorical devices to *reproduce* those worldviews in the reader.

---

22. QR code URL: Ibid.

- The "world in the text" (that is, its narratives) does not equal the "world behind the text" (that is, the real-world history that gives rise to the text), and neither are identical to the "world in front of the text."[23]

- Genre functions: a work's genre communicates, to the competent reader, something of the intent of the text.

- "Dissenting Wisdom" (Job, Ecclesiastes) often sets the bait, so to speak, by laying out tempting morsels of "Conventional Wisdom."

- Complaint against God is a venerable and "live" motif in the Writings.

*"Thoughtfully consider the questions . . ."*

- What do we mean when we say a text "means" something? (Or, how many "meanings" may a text support? Or, where, among text, author, and reader, does "meaning" reside?)

- Does the universe tend toward justice?

- Can conflicting narratives or claims both be "true"?

- Is there such thing as an "innocent," or disinterested, text?

- Can pain or calamity be "solved"? How or how not?

- How does genre help a reader understand a text?

- What is "faith"? Can complaint, or charge of wrongdoing, be "faith"?

- Why do people suffer calamities that they don't deserve?

*"Know and be able to do . . ."*

- Use key terms, including "form and content, setting and function";[24] Writings; Wisdom; "dissenting wisdom and conventional wisdom"; lament psalms; exile; Second Temple; Hellenism.

- Be conversant with major dates beginning with the fall of Jerusalem in 587/586 (539, 515, ca. 450, 332, 167–164).

- Place select locations on a map of the ancient Near East (Mediterranean Sea, Jerusalem, Susa, Euphrates River, city of Babylon, Persian Gulf).

- Describe Walter Brueggemann's approach to genre in the Psalms via "orientation, disorientation, and reorientation."[25]

- Analyze an assigned lament psalm for genre markers.

---

23. Again, Terence E. Fretheim, Gene M. Tucker, and Charles B. Cousar, *The Pentateuch*, Interpreting Biblical Texts (Nashville: Abingdon, 1996), 22–36.

24. John J. Collins helpfully describes "genre" using these terms in "Introduction: Towards the Morphology of a Genre," *Semeia* 14 (1979): 1–19.

25. As described in Walter Brueggemann, *The Psalms and the Life of Faith*, ed. Patrick D. Miller (Minneapolis: Fortress Press, 1995).

- Describe the sociopolitical contexts of early postexilic Yehud and of Seleucid-controlled Jerusalem.

### Stage Two for "OOTLE15"

*"Then you need evidence of the student's ability to . . ."*

- *Explain*: the development and place of the Writings within the HB/OT canon, and of Wisdom within the Writings.

- *Interpret*: two or more texts making markedly competing claims about God and about God's ways in the world, with appropriate attention to the texts' social/historical context. What was bugging each writer, and what did they want to happen in their time?

- *Apply*: Brueggemann's scheme of "orientation, disorientation, and reorientation" to a given lament psalm, with attention to such markers of genre as Address, Statement of Trust, Complaint, Petition, Vow to Offer Thanksgiving.

- *See from the points of view of*: major disputants in the book of Job—Job himself, his wife and friends, Elihu, and God.

- *Empathize with*: sufferers of undeserved calamity, both narrative characters and figures in modern case studies, expressed in informed analysis grounded in the unit's materials and methods.

- *Reflect on*: diversity of perspective as a characteristic of "canon."

Again, this is a good place in the process to draft some rubric boxes. What would it look like to accomplish each of the above tasks excellently, well enough, or not well enough? If you're not sure what "well enough" and "excellently" might look like, ask yourself: How should the assignment be done in order for it to count as compelling evidence of the enduring understandings (big ideas and essential questions) framed in your Stage-One work?

Assessments for OOTLE15 pose a special challenge. My open-Web participants are free to accomplish as much or as little as they choose; they're free agents! And, it would be nice to give them some choices, allowing them some power to shape their curriculum. However, the core group of for-credit Garrett-Evangelical students need to be held accountable for accomplishing such work as justifies a grade in the course. How might I navigate this difference?

One way to simplify assessments for the "core group" is to use a contract grading system. Every assignment is assessed on a pass/fail basis, with the bar set more or less at a "high B" ("good enough and even somewhat better"). At the start of the course, each for-credit student contracts to complete a *certain set* of the whole number of assignments: there is a set for those contracting for an "A," a smaller set for those contracting for a "B," and a still smaller set for those contracting for a "C." A student earns a "D" or an "F" by failing to fill her contracted work on deadline and at passing level. Simplifying things further, I may elect to assess all assignments according to single, simple "all-purpose" assessment rubric used throughout the course.[26]

---

 I describe the contract grading system, and my attraction to it, in this blog post: "Why Don't You Just Tell Me What Grade You Want?"[27]

---

It may be that such a general rubric detracts from the kind of fine-tuning made available in the Stage-Two work above. I'm willing to try it for a semester, and see how it goes. OOTLE15 will be a complex course, and opportunities to simplify expectations and limit time spent on assessment are hard to resist.

### Stage Three for "OOTLE15"

Okay, resources and activities! The contract-grading system means that I would like to have three to four sets of assignments running through the course. For example, each unit might include a close-reading assignment, an assignment relating to historical exegesis, and a fun collaborative activity. Some likely activities, giving students opportunities to accomplish the goals set in Stages One and Two, include:

- Write a blog post from the perspective of one of Job's three friends. Explain and defend your position regarding Job's suffering and his speeches, taking opportunity to distinguish the details of your position from those of the other two friends. Cite appropriately. Help us understand why your position is absolutely the most compelling! Conclude with a reflection on, or response to, God's words in Job 42:7-8. In a follow-up, read blog posts that are "written by" the other two friends, and engage them generously in their comments section. *(You may, if you choose, accomplish this as a YouTube video instead, citing appropriately in the description area.)*

- How, in general terms, does the Chronicler differ from 1–2 Kings, one of his major sources (depiction of David and Solomon, temple and cult, the population of Judah during the exile, etc)? In the person of the Chronicler, describe your social, political, historical context, and write a defense of your choices, with the theme, "Thus-and-so was all very well for 1–2 Kings, but in *my* time this-and-that is going on, so we need to remember things like this!"

---

26. See the appendix, exhibit 2, below, for a current draft of that rubric.
27. QR code URL: http://seminariumblog.org/curator/lesterb201402/.

- In a shared Google Doc, over a twenty-four-hour period, collaborate with all other interested participants in the creation of a lament psalm. You may conspire with others to decide on a specific circumstance for the psalm, but be sure to "hide" any identifying details in a manner appropriate to the psalms. The psalm should include all necessary generic elements, but these may be in *any* order, may be split into different sections or repeated, and may be compressed or extended into any balance. Make a short concluding blog post (or YouTube video), briefly illuminating the psalm through the lens of Brueggemann's "orientation, disorientation, and reorientation." *ALERT: Avoid "defending God" or "explaining" the calamity at hand by means of a theodicy. If it helps, look for inspiration through Psalms 44, 88, and 102.*

Again, once I have my ideas down, I like to assess my plans through the lenses of "WHERETO" and "GRASPS," to be sure that I'm not simply relying on habit in the ways I shape their details.

For my "core group" of for-credit students, I'll choose a shared textbook. Among the important considerations is that the chapters function as independently as possible and that it have a substantive, stand-alone introductory section. If the textbook is instead locked into a fixed ordering, then I won't be able to chop it up according to the needs of my "Bible-backwards" approach. In my experience, Christopher Stanley's introduction has worked well in this regard.[28] For my not-for-credit free participants, I plan to suggest a short list of good, critical introductory textbooks, with advice on finding them through interlibrary loan or cheaply secondhand. Also, each unit will invite learners to engage one or more online resources, many of them topical articles or blog posts.[29]

## Conclusion

Could I possibly have thrown these courses together without Understanding by Design? Yes, of course . . . if I wanted to return to the life that I sketch at the beginning of my introductory chapter. As it is, I am in an enviable position. First, as I craft my assignments in more detail, along with their assessment rubrics (see the appendix, below), I have my Stage-One and Stage-Two notes to serve as a touchstone, keeping me centered on what matters and preventing my planning to skitter away into random directions, especially since I will almost certainly be doing such planning under pressure of a deadline. Second, and as Chris Jones notes in his own work (see ch. 6, below), the "enduring understandings" and "essential questions" crafted in Stage One provide me a touchstone even during the course, as I make (hopefully) minor course corrections in response to actual student performance on

---

28. Christopher D. Stanley, *The Hebrew Bible: A Comparative Approach* (Minneapolis: Fortress Press, 2009).

29. The great trick is to collect such resources all the time, as you come across them. I like to use a social bookmarking tool like Diigo.com to save these. You can see my current collection of candidate resources for OOTLE, https://www.diigo.com/user/blester/ootle.

formative assessments. Third, such "big ideas and essential questions" as I declare to the learners will provide *them* with a clear sense of destination, helping them to focus wisely and avoid needless anxieties about peripheral matters.

You may have gathered that, in what I think is true UbD style, I set a lot of store by Stages One and Two, while holding any Stage-Three plans more lightly. If this makes sense to you by now, then you have a good glimpse of how UbD serves as a "translation tool," allowing me to take the *essence* of a course and transpose it from one learning environment to another (where, perhaps, the resources and activities of the course's current revision are unavailable or impractical). With so many instructors still taking up online and hybrid/blended learning for the first time, it should be clear that this is a particularly inviting application of Understanding by Design. The next chapter examines this more closely: How can UbD serve the face-to-face instructor who is taking her show, for the first time, onto the online-learning road?

## Works Cited

Ben-Porat, Ziva. "The Poetics of Literary Allusion." *PTL: A Journal for Descriptive Poetics and Theory of Literature* 1 (1976): 105–128.

Brueggemann, Walter. *The Psalms and the Life of Faith*. Ed. Patrick D. Miller. Minneapolis: Fortress Press, 1995.

Clawson, Julie. "Self-Inventory on Biblical Hermenuetics." http://julieclawson.com/2010/09/12/self-inventory-on-biblical-hermenuetics/.

Collins, John Joseph. "Introduction: Towards the Morphology of a Genre." *Semeia* 14 (1979): 1–19.

Conte, Gian Biagio, and Charles Segal. *The Rhetoric of Imitation: Genre and Poetic Memory in Virgil and Other Latin Poets*. Cornell Studies in Classical Philology 44. Ithaca: Cornell University Press, 1986.

Fretheim, Terence E., Gene M. Tucker, and Charles B. Cousar. *The Pentateuch*. Interpreting Biblical Texts. Nashville, TN: Abingdon Press, 1996.

Garrett-Evangelical Theological Seminary. "Office of the Registrar: Academic and Program Handbooks." https://mygets.garrett.edu/ICS/Academic_Offices/Office_of_the_Registrar/Academic_and_Program_Handbooks.jnz.

———. "Who We Are." http://www.garrett.edu/who-we-are.

General Board of Higher Education and Ministry. "List of Approved Seminaries." http://www.gbhem.org/education/seminary/approved-seminaries.

Lester, G. Brooke. "Daniel Evokes Isaiah: The Rule of the Nations in Apocalyptic Allusion-Narrative." Unpub. Ph.D. diss., Princeton Theological Seminary, 2008.

———. "Full Reverse! The OT/HB from Writings to Torah." http://seminariumblog.org/curator/lesterb32013/.

———. "Scarcities 2: Online Learning Platforms." http://seminariumblog.org/curator/lesterb82013/.

———. "Why Don't You Just Tell Me What Grade You Want?" http://seminariumblog.org/curator/lesterb201402/.

———. (Bookmarked Web pages tagged "OOTLE.") https://www.diigo.com/user/blester/ootle.

Perri, Carmela. "On Alluding." *Poetics* 7 (1978): 289–307.

Sample, Mark. "Challenging the Presentation Paradigm with the 1/1/5 Rule." http://chronicle
.com/blogs/profhacker/challenging-the-presentation-paradigm-with-the-115-rule.

Stanley, Christopher D. *The Hebrew Bible: A Comparative Approach*. Minneapolis: Fortress
Press, 2009.

Stevens, Dannelle D., and Antonia Levi. *Introduction to Rubrics: An Assessment Tool to Save
Grading Time, Convey Effective Feedback, and Promote Student Learning*. 1st ed. Sterling,
VA: Stylus, 2005.

Wiggins, Grant P., and Jay McTighe. *Understanding by Design Professional Development Workbook*. Alexandria, VA: Association for Supervision and Curriculum Development, 2004.

———. *Understanding by Design*. Exp. 2nd ed. Alexandria, VA: Association for Supervision
and Curriculum Development, 2005.

———, and M. C. Beardsley. "The Affective Fallacy." *The Sewanee Review* 57, (1949): 31–55.

Wimsatt, W. K., Jr. and M. C. Beardsley. "The Intentional Fallacy." *The Sewanee Review* 54,
(1946): 468–488.

Wolcott, Susan K., and C. L. Lynch, "Educator Resources." http://www.wolcottlynch.com
/EducatorResources.html.

# Chapter 4

# Understanding by Design:
# Putting Your Course Online

*G. Brooke Lester*

I t may be that you turned directly to this chapter because you are looking for ways to translate a face-to-face class to some online format. If so, that's fine. Stick with this chapter (I will provide informal cross-references to earlier pages from time to time), and see if it prompts you to investigate the rest of this book as well as Wiggins and McTighe's book, *Understanding by Design*.

It may be that you're already excited about the possibilities of online learning, or maybe find yourself compelled while yet skeptical. Perhaps you have been invited to teach online for the first time (or, been coerced by some means into doing so). Perhaps you have had some experience with online teaching, and it hasn't worked out well. Whatever your trajectory to this point, you stand at the start of a trek into a foreign land. I frequently tell my learners that reading the Bible is *always* a cross-cultural experience. Here, I invite you to see online learning and teaching as a cross-cultural experience—but possibly into a foreign land in which you will elect to establish a permanent residence. Think of it as a second home.

Venturing into this foreign country, you'll naturally be drawn to grasp at any practices or ways of thinking that promise as little change as possible. After all, we are creatures of habit, and it's human nature to try to minimize a change in environment. But you don't make a home in the desert by turning it into the North Woods with which you are more comfortable. You don't adapt to college by insisting it can be just the same as high school. You don't prosper during a student-exchange semester in France by trying to recreate your own home within that of your hosts. Consider the ways that we successfully adapt to new environments:

---

*http://seminariumblog.org/?s=online+learning

(1) we expect culture shock; (2) we become informed; (3) we observe and imitate those prospering in the new environment; (4) we begin integrating the new with the old. This chapter will get you started into this process. If you have friends or colleagues who are already teaching online, and happily, talk with them as much as possible. Find out what they like about it, so that you can begin to imagine experiences, and not just that collection of humiliations that makes up your secret fears about online teaching.

## Clearing the Deck: Some Common Refrains

*"I always have my students do [Activity X]. Can we do [Activity X] online?"*
   The good news is, you probably can. Small-group discussions, debates, student presentations, icebreakers, case studies, role playing—a lot of our favorite classroom activities can be accomplished online. The less-good news is, they are often best accomplished in some form very different from what you know in your face-to-face classroom. For example, it's easy to create two small groups and set them against one another in a formal debate. However, it's much easier to manage this asynchronously, over several days, rather than in some synchronous format. (A synchronous approach—say, using a Google Hangout—has a *much* higher overhead in requisite student skills, bandwidth, and preparation.) But—to get back to good news—the new format imposed on you by the conditions of online learning will come bearing its own gifts. For example, many instructors find that they like asynchronous discussions: comments are more carefully thought through; it's almost impossible for a few students to dominate the discourse; classroom wallflowers tend to blossom.
   From a UbD perspective, though, one is forced to ask: "Why do you assume that you are going to do [Activity X] at all, in the online incarnation of your course?" The resources and activities normal to your face-to-face course are the least important thing about that course. What *really* matters—and you probably know this already, consciously or unconsciously—are the big ideas and essential questions animating the course, and your convictions concerning what a learner must *do* in order to show compelling evidence that they have acquired the enduring understandings representing the goals of the course.
   So, when we translate our face-to-face course into an online environment, we're not packing a bag full of our habitual resources and activities, because they're not actually our beloved children. They are just the children's paraphernalia. Our beloved children are the enduring understandings that animate the course, as we articulate them in our Stage-One and Stage-Two planning in UbD. That's what's going into the travel bag.

*"Online instruction is fine for your course, but my courses aren't just about disseminating information."*
   Believe it or not, but among the *earliest* discoveries of online instruction was that online instruction really doesn't lend itself to one-way disseminating of information—or at least, not in the ways we take for granted in the face-to-face classroom.

In a classroom lecture—"But I don't lecture," somebody interrupts. Okay, but let's be honest, *some* lecturing takes place in any class based on the expertise of the instructor, even if that "lecturing" happens in five-minute increments. If you don't like "lecture," we can call it "telling them things that they don't know." As I was saying: in a classroom telling-them-things-they-don't-know, we rely on nonverbal signals from the hearer, telling us what's getting through and what isn't, and how the material is being received. These nonverbal signals are difficult or impossible to design into online instruction. That's okay—we can design other strategies for feedback—but that's the point: these have to be consciously discovered; they aren't just "there" as they are in the classroom.

In the face-to-face classroom, even where discussion (rather than lecture) dominates, instruction is often largely built around the one-to-one relationships forged between the instructor and each individual student. Imagine the instructor holding the ends of twelve or fifteen (or a hundred) lengths of twine, each extending out to a single student. I remember how my early attempts at "class discussion" reflected this model: Alex comments, I respond; Betsy chimes in, I affirm; Charlotte demurs, I cross-examine; ping-pong, ping-pong, ping-pong.

Hopefully, this is where you tell me how much more sophisticated your handling of classroom interaction is. (And, I promise, I myself have improved.) Here, you instruct me in the ways that you serve as the "Guide on the Side," and not always simply as the "Sage on the Stage." You design activities that stimulate your students' curiosity, and by which your students learn from one another, making subject-matter-related discoveries and integrating them with previous experience. If this is your response, then this is your lucky day, because *this is the shape into which online instruction has naturally developed.*

In online instruction, we "set the table," creating a space that guides learners through meaningful activities both individual and collaborative. Imagine each of the learners holding twelve or fifteen (or a hundred) lengths of twine, the other end of each being held by a peer learner. To the extent that this looks like your best teaching already, or at least your aspirations for teaching, then you are probably going to find that online instruction is, for the most part, already shaped to receive the best of what you have to offer: growing and cultivating communities of inquiry.

Which leads us to . . .

*"'Community' only happens face to face, because of embodiment, and the Incarnation."*

I don't know what the secular parallels to this objection are, but I'm sure they exist—for example, by ending the sentence after "embodiment." But this is how it finds expression in a seminary. I'm going to hit this one pretty hard, because I think there is a whole pack of wolves in this sheep's clothing.

First, assuming that the objector is a teacher, I would ask: "In your classroom, how would *you* approach a *student* who seeks to preemptively shut down an area of inquiry with a thought-terminating cliché?" (Maybe you can find a way to ask this that is less pugnacious and alienating—for tactical reasons, not because the objection warrants the effort.)

Second, assuming that the objector holds a terminal degree in her field of study, I would ask: "What study have you undertaken? What is your body of evidence, and what warrants do you offer for your interpretation of that evidence? Where are the key terms defined?" If the issue of "community" has been raised as a genuine question—and not simply as a kind of theological nuclear option—then the matter warrants inquiry worthy of one holding a research degree.

For my own part, I have found it helpful to take at least an elementary-level sociological approach to the question of "community" in learning. First, what kinds of "community" are there; and second, what are the elements that constitute "community"?

---

 Check out http://www.infed.org/mobi/community/, hosted by George Williams College. It's a site devoted to social pedagogy, defined as "community learning and development," both "informal and nonformal," which leads to social action.[1]

---

Parenthetical note: We all know that there are healthy and unhealthy "communities." But when we talk about "community" as a desideratum, let's agree that the word is shorthand for "*healthy* community." And, while we're at it, we'll remember that even healthy community is not all butterflies and unicorns, but includes dispute, negotiation, and similar gritty realities.

When we are not intoning "community" in hushed tones as some kind of elusive chimera, we take for granted that there are at least three kinds of community. There are, of course, geographic communities, living more or less in some contiguous area. There are also "communities of interest"; examples include the American Academy of Religion and the Society of Biblical Literature; the Audubon Society and United States Chess Federation; Star Trek fans and the attendees of Comic-Con. Finally, there are what the Infed page, cited in the box above, calls communities of "communion," entailing "a profound meeting or encounter," both social and spiritual. If these three kinds of "community" are conflated without reflection, especially "geographic community" and "community of communion," then one could be forgiven the presupposition that "community only happens face to face" (though, even there, is one in geographic community only with those neighbors whom one has seen face to face?). Once these three are distinguished, however, especially including the "communities of interest" that we all accept as naturally distributed, it becomes clear that we cannot simply presuppose that communities even of "communion" happen only face to face. The matter has to be posed as a genuine question.

The same Infed page goes on to examine the constituent elements of "community" (or of "communities"). Among the "norms and habits" of community are

---

1. QR code URL: http://infed.org/mobi/community/.

"tolerance, reciprocity, and trustworthiness." For my own part, I find "tolerance" a grudging word and prefer "acceptance," allowing us a neat mnemonic: Acceptance, Reciprocity, and Trustworthiness. There is an ART to community! In this context, "acceptance" means that everyone gets to be heard. Nobody's experience or ideas are preemptively disallowed. "Reciprocity" means that I'll do for you now without immediate reward, confident that you (or someone else in the group) will come through for me when I need it down the line. "Trustworthiness" means consistency, reliability, both on the part of teaching staff and fellow students. You know that experiment where they drive dogs crazy by rewarding and punishing them arbitrarily and unpredictably? "Trustworthiness" is the opposite.

I'm not sure how to measure "community" in a classroom. But I'll bet you (and your learners, for that matter) can come up with ways to assess the learning space for Acceptance, Reciprocity, and Trustworthiness. Now, when the question comes up as to whether this happens only "face to face," where there is "embodiment" (I'm going to let the Incarnation take care of itself), we can point to *actual instances of online courses* and frame it as a question: Are the elements of community present or not, and how so, and how do we know, and what might be done about it? This is messier than a thought-stopping cliché, and therefore undoubtedly closer to reflecting the truth of the situation.

*"I need to be able to see all their faces."*
For starters, let's observe urgently that *any* utterance beginning with "I need . . ." reflects, by definition, a teacher-centered approach to course design. It's natural, habitual, insidious: I'm asked to teach a course, and right away I ask myself, "What do I need to teach this material? Let's see, I'll need lecture notes, I'll need a textbook that jibes with my approach to the material, I'll need to decide on where to 'cap' enrollment numbers, I need, I need." Understanding by Design sits solidly among the learner-centered approaches to creating courses. *What does the learner need in order to come to the enduring understandings that animate my aspirations for the course?* Do they "need" for me to "see all their faces"? To what ends, exactly? (I don't pose the question rhetorically as a ploy to shut the matter down, I'm just inviting the objector to imagine the objection as a genuine question rather than as an assertion.)

It is a good question, because the idea that teaching involves "seeing all their faces" is (in my experience) the most common presupposition instructors who are thinking of undertaking online teaching for the first time raise. Accompanying this is the similar presupposition that synchronous learning activities are inherently preferable to asynchronous activities. The good news is that the technical, financial, and logistical obstacles to an all-synchronous, all-faces-all-the-time online learning space remain effectively insuperable. I call this "good news" because—as the very existence of this chapter implies—any attempt simply to recreate online the conditions of face-to-face learning are not only doomed to failure ("technical, financial, and logistical obstacles"), but would tragically insulate the instructor and students from the unique and often unpredictable possibilities for learning offered by the online environment.

A story: My very first online course had (mercifully) a simple structure that I inherited from the faculty member who had designed it: a Blackboard learning-management system with discussion forums and a pretty nifty "virtual classroom" allowing weekly, one-hour synchronous engagement. Often, after our weekly synchronous conference, one or more students would hang back and chat informally with me for a while. One week, a student I'll call "Laura" hung back and told me that this wasn't her first online course, and that she was enjoying our course more than most. Unlike her previous instructors, I had not invited students to post photographs of themselves as part of their introductory "ice-breaker" forum posts. (The truth is, I had agreed to teach the course at the eleventh hour, and it simply hadn't occurred to me to ask for them in pursuit of a closer "community.") Laura told me that she was glad I hadn't asked them to post pictures. In our course, she said, "Everyone treats me as if I were pretty."

Take a moment on that, if you like. I won't say I have since never invited the inclusion of photos in online learner profiles. But I certainly appreciate, in a way I didn't before, that the matter is a lot more complicated than my own reflexive, habitual, teacher-centered notions about what "I need." The moral is not to never use photos. It is that these teacher-centered dogmatic claims ("I need . . .") have to be interrogated by student experience, and are always contingent to the possibility of unanticipated student need.

## A Linear Guide to the Iterative Process of Translation

Understanding by Design is teleological in shape: Stage One necessitates Stage Two, which calls ineluctably for Stage Three. At the same time, you are not coming in as a tabula rasa. Read through what follows, and find the entry point that suits your temperament and whatever collection of tools and experience you bring to the process.

UbD is best done on a unit-by-unit basis. Your course as a whole is too big and unwieldy to design in one fell swoop. Designing session by session is, it goes without saying, obviously no solution. If you have not already, try to divide your course into logical units, four or five of them perhaps. Pick one that excites you or seems to be a "crux" in the course, and get to work designing that. Believe me, the first one is the hardest, and the others will fall into place fairly easily afterwards.

### Stage Zero: Create a Learner Profile

If you happen to have experience with crafting sermons, you'll know that there is no answer to that most common of student questions, "But Prof, how does this preach?" A sermon is a unique event marking the intersection, not only of preacher and text, but of preacher, text, hearers, and the long-term and more acute circumstances of those hearers. (We may as well throw in the circumstances of the preacher as well.)

Just so with an educational experience. We can't ask, "Here is my subject matter, so how does it teach?" unless we take into account the peculiarities of the learners.

Learners contribute to the educational experience no less than do the instructor and the subject matter. (Troublesome, aren't they?) Even if I feel like I already know my institution's student body, my perceptions are filtered through whatever racket habitually reverberates in my head at this point in my interactions with them. Better to take an inventory.

Write up what you know about your learners. Want it to go easily? Start with a list, "Things that drive me crazy about our students." You might supplement that same list with, "Things I just always wish regarding our students." Got that all out of your system? Now: "Okay, things I really actually like very much about our students, especially on my good days." Finally, try to specify: "Misunderstandings and faulty presuppositions common to our students." This is a good minimum. For practical aspects (their computer savvy, accessibility to Internet, etc.), see the "Learner Profile" in the previous chapter.

## Stage One: Develop Objectives

In order to avoid a lot of repetition from the last chapter, I'm just going to show you the basic formulae in Stage One and Stage Two. If you do some good-faith brainstorming just off the top of your head, that will be enough to help you wrap your mind around the process that we're talking about here.[2]

The overall formula for Stage One is, "If the desired result is for the learners to *meet certain grade standards* (G); to have certain *understandings* (U); to consider given *essential questions* (Q); and to *know* certain facts and have certain *skills* (KS) . . ." Taking it a piece at a time:

*"Meet the Standards . . ."* What goals does your institution express for its graduates? Mission statements and degree-program goals may often be rather vague and generalized (why do we think that this makes for good promotional copy?), but can be mined for evocative concepts ("bold leaders"!). If yours is a public school, you may have well-defined standards in place. Print them out, circle or highlight any that excite you or toward which your subject matter plainly makes you accountable. Again, look for keywords or catchphrases that you can use later as a "lens" through which to assess the brainstorming you do in Stages Two and Three.

*"Understand that . . ."* Think of your conversations with faculty peers or with your sympathetic family. "I wish that they better understood that . . ." "Oh my gosh, if they don't 'get' X, then how can they 'get' everything else?" "I'll put up with a lot on the final exam, but they have to demonstrate an appreciation that . . ." Write these down. Avoid "facts" (the date of the division of the United Monarchy; that Israel is the one in the North and Judah the one in the South). Assuming that they can look up "facts" whenever they want, what do they need to *understand* in order to be motivated to make the effort? What must they understand in order not to

---

2. The quotes in the following draw on the language of Grant Wiggins and Jay McTighe, *Understanding by Design*, exp. 2d ed. (Alexandria, VA: Association for Supervision and Curriculum Development, 2005).

butcher them when they do look them up? Write down every "understanding" you can think of.

*"Thoughtfully consider the questions . . ."* A good essential question is one that has no definite answer. I don't mean that the answer is *unknown* (like, the current exact size in meters of the perimeter of Lake Michigan). I mean that the question is one for which competing answers may be proposed. A question that breeds other questions that breed other questions. For example, "What is the good life?" "Why do humans fight?" See where you can make them unit-specific: "What makes prophecy 'true'?" Draw on your understandings above, or drift freely (perhaps with your old syllabi in view).

*"Know and be able to do . . ."* This is a good opportunity to consider the "brass tacks" of content (or, sigh, "coverage"). What facts *do* they need to control in order to do the higher-level stuff to which you'd like them to aspire in this unit? What basic skills (writing, speaking, interacting) are required?

### Stage Two: Build Assessment Rubrics

Return to the formula, picking up where Stage One left off: ". . . then I need evidence of the student's ability to" demonstrate the Six Facets of Understanding: Explanation, Interpretation, Application, Perspective, Empathy, Reflection.

At the conclusion of the unit at hand, what should your learners be able to explain clearly? What texts or situations ought they to be able to interpret using the tools acquired? What methods or practices do you want to see them apply (and to what?). Whose perspectives (whether historical figures, literary characters, or actual populations) ought they to be prepared to represent accurately? With whom would you like them to show empathy in consideration of the big ideas and essential questions animating the unit? What reflections suggest themselves as a fruitful use of their time?

Start imagining how such performances might be assessed. Don't sweat the details yet with regard to these as "assignments" (Are they done in three-page papers, or discussion forums, or via interpretive dance, or . . . ?). Just write some ideas about what it would look like to, say, "Explain X" in an exemplary way, or to "Apply method Y to text or case study Z." What, specifically, would make such performances "More than Good Enough, or Good Enough, or Not Good Enough" in terms of allowing you to "catch" the learner in the act of showing the desired enduring understandings?

Again, these are not built around imagined activities (papers, discussions, etc.). That comes later. These are built around such *demonstrations* that would provide *compelling evidence* that a learner has achieved the *enduring understandings* embodied in your big ideas and essential questions.

### Pause, Observe: That's It—That's Your "Travel Kit."

Big ideas and essential questions, and a corresponding good start on assessment rubrics: that's the core of your course. Think of it like the travel bag kept, always ready, by the frequent traveler. When you revise your course for a new institution, a changing student body, some fresh insights on the subject matter, simply work up a fresh learner profile and continue with the following steps.

### Imagining Stage Three: Consider the Environment

How simple can it be? What is and isn't available in the default environment as you receive it: linked files, discussion forums, online quizzes/exams, space for multimedia files and means for playing them, glossaries and wikis, and so forth? How closed must it be (how open can it be)? What are people used to? List the tools that are available, that you've used or not used. Try to think in binaries: synchronous and asynchronous; textual and multimedia; individual and collaborative; open (public) and closed (private). The goal is to develop a list of those tools that are most readily available and with which you are most comfortable (already, or potentially). Will your learners be able to purchase commercial resources like a shared textbook, or will you be putting together a "course pack" that respects copyrights?

Do a little research (this will often mean, "Ask people who might know"): What sorts of educational activities have other instructors managed using these tools? For example, take the humble discussion forum: if you ask around, you will find instructors who use them for introductions/"icebreakers" and for simple discussion ("Discuss the reading and respond to three peers"), but also for week-long formal team debates, for "snowball" discussions (an asynchronous form of think-pair-share-square), "fishbowl" discussions, as a hub for various collaborative projects, role plays, and more.

Note: This is where an online-learning certification course or program can be especially valuable. It's not really about learning to manage the tools technologically. After all, tools and environments come and go (that's the conviction driving this chapter!). Ideas about the innumerable ways one can "hack" on a tool to derive unexpected uses out of it is a mindset, and a contagious one. The more excitement you can generate about drawing on the cultural capital already out there, the more creatively you will be able to add to the pool.

### Stage Three: Resources and Activities

Now it's time to do the familiar part—and that's the danger. It would be easy here simply to select from among your habitual resources and activities, adapted minimally for the online environment. It *may* be that many of them will work, but try to consider each one guilty until proven innocent: Will it allow the learner to accomplish the performances described in your assessment rubrics? Only if the answer is "Yes" does it have a place.

Don't be afraid to keep it simple. There's no virtue in using exotic or baroque tools where a simpler solution is available. Let's say you build your course in a standard learning-management system (LMS) like Blackboard or Moodle, and that you limit things to (1) a textbook and some PDF articles, (2) discussion forums, and (3) uploaded papers. Such a course can be richly imaginative and promote deep learning, *if* these readings and assignments permit the learner to do what's asked in your planned assessments, and thereby provide evidence of the enduring understandings around which you have designed the course. Conversely, a course could be stuffed with relatively edgy and exciting tools (say, Twitter chats, Google Hangouts, a wiki, public blogging—all of which are frequently used with terrific results), and by its failure to link in with Stage-One and Stage-Two design work, produce little or nothing in the way of enduring understandings. Make the simplest choices that you can make with integrity, because—let's face it—things will go wrong, the unexpected will happen, and housekeeping will demand about thrice the time you expect.

So, then, what *will* you do when, in the first days and weeks of your online course, the wheels seem like to come off the wagon? First, you'll remind your learners what you told them at the start of the course: *"Be patient with us, and we'll be patient with you. When things seem to break down unexpectedly, don't worry, we won't hold you accountable for the impossible."* (Oh, yeah: Don't forget to have told them that.) Second, having now paid your dues, you'll receive your membership card and jacket, having now joined The Club. (Our secret handshake is a tired shrug.) And, third, you will Trust the Design. A *lot* can go wrong, but you know that the caravan is moving in the right direction: toward the performances that give evidence of relevant, enduring understandings. What do a few pitstops and safaris along the route matter, except as unexpected opportunities for discovery?

Your online course is complete. Grades are in. Take out your UbD pocket knife, and cut the course, with all of its Stage-Three resources and activities, loose. Leave it behind as a monument to the victory you have shared with your learners. Like a ninja, or a backpacker, you travel light. Keep your duffel slung over your shoulder, holding your Stage-One and Stage-Two course-building toiletry kit, and stroll confidently into the sunset and toward your next adventure.

## Works Cited

Wiggins, Grant P., and Jay McTighe. *Understanding by Design Professional Development Workbook.* Alexandria, VA: Association for Supervision and Curriculum Development, 2004.
———. *Understanding by Design.* Exp. 2nd ed. Alexandria, VA: Association for Supervision and Curriculum Development, 2005.

# Chapter 5

# Understanding by Design: New Testament at University

*Jane S. Webster*

U nderstanding by Design provides an extremely useful matrix for us to think about our course design in the liberal-arts context, for it requires us to identify explicitly what we think adults should understand, know, and do by the time they complete a course. More than that, UbD invites us to think beyond the bounds of our own discipline and urges us to consider an understanding that is enduring and that extends beyond the walls and the moment of the classroom. It pushes us to press past the memorization of factual content into the realm of a deeper knowing, and with that, an enactment of such knowing into creative and critical thinking. It should be a staple in higher education. Unfortunately, instructors in institutions of higher education rarely design their curriculum and particular courses this way.

We are not trained to teach. We acquired our own education by knowing who said what about what and why it was important; we achieved expert status by saying something new in a new way. If we are lucky and work hard, we may find our way into a faculty position. As new teachers, we usually follow the models of our own instructors and mentors: we "cover content" that lays the foundations of the discipline and introduces students to the ongoing conversation carried on by our predecessors. But when students are not as interested as we hoped, or don't work as hard and learn as much as we expect, then we realize that we might need to learn how to teach differently.

And teaching is so complex! We simultaneously need to hold our knowledge and understanding of the principles of biblical studies, the requirements of the curriculum, the social, intellectual, and developmental needs of our students, and

*http://seminariumblog.org/author/jane-s-webster/

the time we have left in our schedule; at the same time, we need to analyze what students comprehend and where they get stuck, and determine how we can best lead them to understanding. It's mind boggling! Thankfully, we don't need to figure it all out at once; we can add one layer at a time, and hopefully, with practice, these skills will become more automatic.[1]

In this part of the book, I will apply Understanding by Design specifically to biblical-studies courses in the undergraduate liberal-arts context. I will start by defining the context and the place of biblical studies in the curriculum, and move into the complex interface of competing curriculum goals. I will follow this with a description of how I lay out the basic framework of any course in biblical studies using Understanding by Design, followed by an explicit example of a 200-level "Introduction to the New Testament" course that I teach at Barton College in North Carolina.

## What the Teaching Context Demands

"Teaching the Bible" means different things in different contexts. In churches and synagogues, people teach the Bible in order to generate awe and wonder for the divine, to build community around a common narrative and ideology, and to identify ethical principles. They often avoid questions about authorship and historical context, and read instead for the "confessional" purposes of nurturing the faithful, or for the theological purposes of understanding the nature and ways of God. Teachers in seminaries might introduce questions and controversies in the Bible, but they generally train their students for sermon preparation and for ecclesiastical, theological, and ethical debate. Teachers in university graduate schools linger over the controversies and debates focusing more on the sociohistorical or literary features of the text; they generally eschew confessional and theological agendas. Teachers of the Bible in liberal-arts colleges have a very different task at hand.

Teachers in liberal arts colleges generally aim to prepare students academically for entry into career paths, and in some cases, professional and graduate schools. Their colleges traditionally offer undergraduate degrees (a four-year program usually leads to a Bachelors of Science or Art) and a residential setting, so these teachers work mainly with young people aged seventeen to twenty who come for the "full college experience": they have left home for the first time, are developing new social networks, and are generally "growing up." These teachers will also encounter students in their classrooms who do not fit the "traditional" profile, such as those who enter college later in life or are military veterans or commuting students.

Teachers in the liberal arts often contribute to the general education curriculum, which is designed to promote certain proficiencies; Barton College, as but one example, requires students to demonstrate competencies in computer use, calculation (mathematics), composition, critical thinking (in laboratory science and social science), physical fitness, and global awareness. Teachers of religion usually

---

1. For an inventory of all that goes through an expert teacher's mind while teaching, see Magdalene Lampert, *Teaching Problems and the Problems of Teaching* (New Haven: Yale University Press, 2001).

find themselves contributing to this global-awareness "basket" by helping students to become more knowledgeable of the traditions that shape culture. Those who teach biblical-studies courses, more specifically, lead students to understand the ways in which the Bible influences Western culture and, in turn, how its interpretation is influenced by culture.[2] As is the case in many institutions, teachers of religion courses must also teach skills, such as writing, critical thinking, or oral communication.

Unlike their colleagues at a Bible college or seminary, teachers in the liberal arts often face a more ambivalent group of students. While an occasional student will sign on as a religion major (usually as a second major), most students will take religion courses as part of the general education requirements. Some will elect a biblical-studies course because they "have been to church their whole life" and they expect the course will be a more sophisticated Sunday school class. Others take the course because it "was the only one that fit their schedule." Some know the Bible well; others feel at a distinct disadvantage because they know nothing. Some students enter the course girded against "the loss of their faith" predicted by their pastors, determined "to set the professor straight" and "to testify to God's faithfulness." Some students, especially those of other faith traditions, are intellectually curious about what the Bible says. Very few students have ever studied the Bible in an academic environment. Teachers in biblical studies thus need to be both attentive and empathetic to the previous knowledge, skills, expectations, and commitments that these students bring into their classroom.

Teachers in liberal-arts undergraduate colleges also face a wide array of cognitive ability among their students, especially with respect to what students perceive to be the nature and acquisition of knowledge, or "truth."[3] William Perry provides a helpful analysis of the different stages of development. When students first enter college, he claims, they believe that knowledge is fixed and stable, either right or wrong, good or bad, "this or that." They trust the authority of their parents and teachers, and seek to acquire knowledge by gathering information. Eventually, students will move into the second stage—contextual relativism—when they realize that truth "all depends" on the context, that truth is "constructed"; they think, "maybe this or maybe that." The latter stages of development, which Perry calls "commitment," occur when students integrate knowledge learned from others with their own experience and develop commitments to particular points of view on differing topics; they are open to rethinking their commitments if evidence arises that

---

2. Although Barton College (formerly Atlantic Christian College) has its roots in the Disciples of Christ (Christian) Church, and religion courses were once central to the curriculum, religion courses are no longer required of all students.

3. See William G. Perry Jr., *Forms of Intellectual and Ethical Development in the College Years—A Scheme* (New York: Holt, Rinehart and Winston, 1968); "Cognitive and Ethical Growth: The Making of Meaning," in Arthur W. Chickering and Associates, *The Modern American College: Responding to the New Realities of Diverse Students and a Changing Society* (San Francisco: Jossey-Bass, 1981), 76–116; Patrick G. Love and Victoria L. Guthrie, *Understanding and Applying Cognitive Development Theory: New Directions for Student Services* (San Francisco: Jossey-Bass, 1999). See "William Perry's Scheme of Intellectual and Ethical Development," http://www.jmu.edu/geology/evolutionarysystems/protected/handouts/willperry2.pdf.

has merit; they balance one commitment with another. They think, "sometimes this, sometimes that." When teachers meet students who are struggling to work through competing authorities and truth claims in their biblical-studies classes, they also meet a range of student responses—uncritical acceptance, resistance, or thoughtful reflection; and they often have to negotiate with students in the same classroom who are functioning at different levels of cognitive development.

Consequently, teachers of biblical-studies courses in the undergraduate liberal-arts context face distinct challenges. They must teach the Bible as a cultural arti-fact, respecting the students who give it authority, those who do not, and those who question its authority. They must lay the foundations of biblical studies for the religion major, but keep the course relevant for less-invested nonmajors. They may also need to address larger curricular concerns, such as global awareness or technical skills. Finally, they must balance these demands to create a space where all students have an opportunity to learn. Teaching biblical studies in the liberal-arts context is complex indeed.

## What Students Want to Learn

Most teachers learn that they cannot teach something to someone who does not really want to learn it, but that doesn't keep them from trying. They might attempt to entertain their students into curiosity, playing funky music, showing clips from *The Simpsons*, or telling jokes. They might appeal to various learning styles, invit-ing students to act out a biblical narrative, to engage community-service learning, or to compare forms of art. They might attempt to motivate their students with grades or win their students' hearts by being kind. Teachers expend a lot of energy trying to motivate their students to learn. UbD suggests that teachers spend more time identifying what students want to learn, and why they want to learn it.[4]

According to several studies, many students use their college years to figure out who they are and where they are going. Sharon Daloz Parks, for example, claims that young people attempt to make meaning of experiences, beliefs, and values, but also to reflect on, test, and transform them.[5] In an extensive seven-year study, Alex-ander Astin, Helen Astin, and Jennifer Lindholm found that students' *"spiritual growth enhances other college outcomes*, such as academic performance, psychologi-cal well-being, leadership development, and satisfaction with college."[6] Of several opportunities that have the greatest impact on student spiritual growth, such as study abroad and service learning, they identified the importance of interdisciplin-ary studies, self-reflection, and conversations about the meaning and purpose of life. College students thus seek to understand themselves and where they fit into the world; they see their college education as an opportunity—a rite of passage—to

---

4. See Maryellen Weimer's *Learner-Centered Teaching: Five Key Changes to Practice* (San Francisco: Jossey-Bass, 2002) for ways to focus on student needs rather than the faculty's needs.
5. Parks refers to this as "faith development." Sharon Daloz Parks, *Big Questions, Worthy Dreams: Men-toring Young Adults in Their Search for Meaning, Purpose, and Faith* (San Francisco: Jossey-Bass, 2000), 10.
6. Alexander Astin, Helen Astin, and Jennifer Lindholm, *Cultivating the Spirit: How College Can Enhance Students' Inner Lives* (San Francisco: Jossey-Bass, 2011), emphasis original, 10.

transition from adolescent to adult. And they often seek to work through these questions in biblical-studies courses.[7]

---

This QR code points to the First Amendment Center's "A Teacher's Guide to Religion in the Public Schools" by Charles C. Haynes.[8]

---

Most biblical scholar-teachers, however, avoid these conversations. They respect the spirit of the First Amendment that states that "Congress shall make no law respecting an establishment of religion, or prohibiting the free exercise thereof": students can exercise freedom of religion and if a teacher appears to promote one religion over another, or to raise questions with which students are uncomfortable, then students will disengage or complain. As a result, instructors teach *about* religion objectively, and leave the students to fend for themselves in their questions of personal identity, meaning, and purpose. But like it or not, teachers of the Bible provoke life questions because of the very nature of the discipline, sending students to seek answers outside of the classroom, hopefully with guidance from their spiritual leaders or religious groups. If students actually want to discuss questions of spiritual quest in their biblical-studies classes, might teachers design a course backward to meet those learning goals?

---

See this recent article, in which Marshall Poe argues that colleges should create space for pastors to teach spiritual practices—the knowledge-how of religion, rather than the knowledge-that of religion—to help students cope. "Colleges Should Teach Religion to Their Students: When students feel adrift, spiritual guidance might help."[9]

---

Students are also highly motivated to develop the skills they will need in order to get and keep a job, skills such as the ability to work in teams with different types of people, to write and speak well, to solve complex problems, to understand the global context, or to apply knowledge and skills to new settings. They understand that what they can do (transferable skills), rather than what they know (content knowledge), will keep them more flexible in emerging job markets and global

---

7. See Barbara E. Walvoord, *Teaching and Learning in College Introductory Religion Courses* (Malden, MA: Wiley-Blackwell, 2008).

8. QR code URL: http://www.firstamendmentcenter.org/madison/wp-content/uploads/2011/03/teachers guide.pdf.

9. QR code URL: http://www.theatlantic.com/education/archive/2014/03/colleges-should-teach -religion-to-their-students/284296.

environments.[10] If they know they are acquiring these useful skills in a biblical-studies course, they are more likely to engage enthusiastically. Again, teachers can design their course backward to develop a targeted skill.

 For a list of skills that employers desire in new college graduates, see Liberal Education and America's Promise (LEAP) Web site:[11]

In any case, a teacher will more likely get student "buy-in" if they consider what the students themselves would like to understand.

## Enduring Understandings or Metaquestions?

Perhaps the most challenging aspect of backward design is to determine an enduring understanding that can be taught well with biblical-studies content, especially in a context where the Bible is neither interesting nor authoritative for all students. In a Bible college or seminary, an enduring understanding might be, "The Bible encourages us to forgive others and act with justice," or "God acts in mysterious ways," or "Jesus provides a model for living well." In a graduate school, an enduring understanding might be, "Understanding the past helps us to understand the present," or "Interpretation of a text must consider the context in which it was generated," or "Meaning is found at the junction of the reader and the text." These types of understandings are a hard sell in the liberal-arts context because they will appeal to only a very few members of the group, engaging some but leaving others out in the cold. A course should focus on an enduring understanding that will intrigue most, if not all, students in the course.

One enduring understanding that engages most students in a liberal-arts undergraduate context is related to the notion of biblical literacy. In *Religious Literacy: What Every American Needs to Know—And Doesn't*, Stephen Prothero lists important religious ideas and motifs that predominate in Western culture.[12] Courses that focus on biblical literacy help students to identify and to understand the basis of Western assumptions, and so to understand those who are informed by them. For example, by studying the Bible, students will learn that cultures based on the Bible value the trickster (Jacob, David), the "one who dies for many" (Jesus), and deferred justice (heaven and hell). Is this urgent? Jacques Berlinerblau thinks so. While observing that "secularists are free to remain oblivious" to religious traditions,

---

10. "Despite the transformations in the world of higher education, there have been only a few changes in learning strategies and instruction methods." See Nitza Davidovitch, "Learning-Centered Teaching and Backward Course Design: From Transferring Knowledge To Teaching Skills," *Journal of International Education Research* 9, no. 4 (2013): 330.

11. QR code URL: http://www.aacu.org/leap/students/employerstopten.cfm.

12. Stephen Prothero, *Religious Literacy: What Every American Needs to Know about Religion—and Doesn't* (New York: HarperCollins, 2007).

he warns that "now is *not* the best time to exercise this freedom."[13] Whether secularists like it or not, religious people are still in the majority; if we ignore religious literacy, we do so at our peril: "One flinch and secularists everywhere may have the opportunity to experience the end of days right along with the euphoric faithful."[14] When religious fundamentalism threatens global peace, even our very existence, indifference to religion is not a viable option. More specifically, he argues that "in a society where interpretations of the Bible routinely affect the lives of all citizens, learning how to criticize claims made on behalf of the Bible is a useful civic virtue."[15] Thus, he argues that all people should understand that the Bible is not univocal, nor are its interpreters; he says, "In response to the fanatic's self-assertion that 'The Bible says this!' the intellectual responds, 'Well, maybe not'. . . . They infect the social body with doubt . . . [and provide] countless reasons to hesitate before acting on the Bible's behalf."[16] Both Berlinerblau and Prothero argue that biblical literacy is an urgent student learning outcome.

Along these lines, one related enduring understanding in biblical-studies courses might be that "biblical literacy helps people to identify subtle cultural coercion." In order to arrive at this understanding, students would need to know the following:

1. A range of biblical motifs in narrative, image, and character;

2. The possible sociohistorical context that generated the motif;

3. The presence of biblical motifs in a transformed context.

They would need to do the following:

1. Identify and evaluate rhetorical strategies;

2. Test the "truth"-claims of biblical motifs in popular culture;

3. Construct an argument for or against the appropriate use of a biblical motif in popular culture.

Regardless of their religious status, students gain knowledge: they have the opportunity to examine "objectively" both an ancient and a modern cultural artifact, to identify the influence of the Bible in Western culture,[17] to build foundational knowledge in the discipline (necessary for religion majors), and to identify principles of interpretation. They develop cognitively: they experience the familiar as strange and the strange as familiar, and evaluate claims of truth and authority.

---

13. Jacques Berlinerblau, *The Secular Bible: Why Non-believers Must Take Religion Seriously* (New York: Cambridge University Press, 2005), 1 (emphasis added).

14. Ibid., 2.

15. Ibid., 112.

16. Ibid., 117.

17. For specific examples on this, see Dee Dyas and Esther Hughes, *The Bible in Western Culture: The Student's Guide* (New York: Routledge, 2005); or Cullen Schippe and Chuck Stetson, eds., *The Bible and Its Influence* (New York: Bible Literacy Project, 2006); Mark Roncase and Patrick Gray, eds., *Teaching the Bible: Practical Strategies for Classroom Instruction* (Atlanta: Society of Biblical Literature, 2005); idem, *Teaching the Bible through Popular Culture and the Arts* (Atlanta: Society of Biblical Literature, 2007); T. J. Wray, *What the Bible Really Tells Us: The Essentials Guide to Biblical Literacy* (New York: Rowman and Littlefield, 2011).

They develop spiritually: they begin to cultivate a sense of their identity and purpose by considering what they allow to define and influence them. They develop skills of problem solving, critical thinking, and writing. As the enduring understanding shapes the course, many "traditional objectives" will still be realized but the objectives are learner-centered rather than discipline- or faculty-centered.

Here are some other possibilities of enduring understandings for a biblical-studies course in the undergraduate liberal-arts setting:

- Each religion that draws from the Bible defends its faith, in part, by a selective, human interpretation of the key Bible passages from which the faith springs.

- It is difficult to reconcile the literalist view of the Bible with a historical understanding of the text(s) as written by many men over many years.

- One need not believe in the God of the Bible to appreciate the power of image, language, and history in the text and the influence of the text on all the arts from the time it was written.

While some students will be drawn to these "big ideas," other students will be less intrigued, thinking the Bible altogether irrelevant. But many will be drawn to the *metaquestions* that lie behind the understandings, questions that they themselves are already asking and which all people in all contexts ask themselves at one time or another. Here are some examples:

- What does it mean to be alive?

- How do we stay safe in the midst of unpredictability?

- What is a good life?

- Why do we suffer?

- What happens to "me" when I die?

- How do we get along with other people?

- Why are we different?

- Are we alone?

- What is truth?

- Where does authority come from?

Most students will resonate with these bigger questions and be invested in solving them in their own way at some level; they might already be familiar with ways that people answer these questions in their biology, psychology, or literature courses. Yet to see these questions arise in biblical-studies courses, students see the silos of the discipline fall down; they realize that their education in one field has relevance in another; they develop flexibility and breadth in their own understanding. Therefore, instead of taking a course in Bible, students take a course in a metaquestion, examining various solutions that the Bible has to offer and comparing them to other solutions they may have previously encountered. Students are then left to judge for themselves whether the solutions the Bible presents are reasonable or useful. The teacher can also tap into students' personal experience, lead them to reflect and to reconsider their current understanding, and add layers of meaning to the already-familiar. An added bonus is that the teacher steps back as the dispenser of authoritative opinions or as a counterauthority to their parents and other teachers, and becomes, in the eyes of the students perhaps, a fellow pilgrim in the quest to discover identity, meaning, and purpose.

In a course on the "Life and Teaching of Jesus," for example, we might ask the question, "What is truth?" Students might work through various presentations of Jesus, such as the Synoptic Gospels, John, the letters of Paul, Hebrews, Revelation, extracanonical Gospels, Jesus- or Christ-figure films, art, and literature. They would learn the content in the discipline (foundational knowledge), and how to determine what is true (cognitive development), to identify to what or to whom they give authority (self-actualization), to identify, analyze, arrange, evaluate, and interpret evidence (critical thinking), and to describe their results effectively and persuasively (communication, rhetoric). They do not need to "cover all the content," but can examine in some depth selected divergent examples. In these ways, students can engage their own question—What is truth?—using the content of the biblical-studies course.[18]

The benefits of backward design may be met at the college level, in my experience, more satisfactorily with a metaquestion than with an enduring understanding. Related to big ideas, the metaquestion gives the course design coherence and direction, but, rather than aiming for a particular understanding, students have more freedom to explore the edges of various solutions, to draw their own conclusions, and to gain autonomy in understanding. They will also begin to make those cognitive shifts from "this or that" thinking to "sometimes this, sometimes that" thinking, but they will make those shifts, not out of conflict and confrontation, but through curiosity and discovery.

## Adapting Course Design for Liberal-Arts Colleges

The practice of a biblical-studies course design might feel quite daunting at this point. There are so many things to consider! In what follows, I will describe the steps of Understanding by Design as I have adapted them over years of tweaking and reworking for multiple courses in religious and biblical studies in the undergraduate liberal-arts context. After a description of the general steps—which can be used for any course—I will describe the design decisions I made for a specific course in New Testament.

---

18. For specific examples, see Jane S. Webster, "Teaching with Meta-Questions," or Russell C. D. Arnold, "Course Design and the Use of Meta-Questions in an Interdisciplinary First-Year Seminar on the Ethics of Biblical Interpretation," both in *Teaching the Bible in the Liberal Arts Classroom*, ed. Jane S. Webster and Glenn S. Holland (Sheffield, UK: Sheffield Phoenix, 2012), 217–22; 223–32.

### Step 1. Identify an Enduring Understanding or a Metaquestion

Identify either an enduring understanding or a metaquestion around which you will design your course. An understanding or question, you will recall, should be open-ended, multidimensional, addressed in various disciplines (to promote transfer skills and flexible learning), relevant to the students in the classroom (consider age, cognitive development, experience, and context), and promote personal meaning-making. Ask: What do students need to understand?

### Step 2. Identify Ways to Know That Your Students Understand: Summative Assessment

What will students learn to do? Imagine a product of some kind with which students can demonstrate that they have acquired the understanding or have explored the multidimensions of the question: we will call this product a "summative assessment." The possibilities are endless, and need not look like the standard essay or exam. In making your selection, consider a variety of factors, including what your own particular context and skills might have to offer:

- *Consider the level of study and where this course fits into the overall curriculum*: Is it a foundational course, an honors course, a writing-intensive, or a senior capstone? Do you need to assess individual skills or develop teamwork? Do you need to build research skills? Do you want to integrate service learning or study abroad? Do you need to teach a specific learning objective, such as writing or critical thinking? These factors will have an impact on the design of your summative assessment.

- *Decide what genre your summative assessment should take*. What type of work product makes sense at this cognitive level, for this project, for the discipline of biblical studies, and for the types of majors in your course? Consider, for example, a platform speech, a presentation, a poster session, a research essay, an executive summary, a promotional pamphlet, a short story, a monologue, a screenplay, a documentary, or a work of art. Encourage students to determine effective features of the genre by scrutinizing several examples. Connect this genre concretely with their potential careers to give them more incentive to learn the skill. Alternatively, consider giving students a choice of genre.

- *Consider the audience for the project*. When students know that their work will be evaluated by a "real audience," they will usually set the bar a little higher for themselves. They look to their teachers as collaborators rather than evaluators, and receive feedback more readily because they do not want to embarrass themselves. In preparation, they will need to identify their audience's attitudes, beliefs, assumptions, cultural practices, and professional standards. For example, they might consider as the audience a community organization, a political or religious figure, or a professional group. As much as possible, therefore, find a way to shift the "final assessment" beyond the bounds of the classroom so that students will have practice and build confidence through engaging in the authentic expectations of the professional world.

- *Consider what makes your personal work interesting.* Can you draw students into your own research projects? Can you find a way to engage students in real-work projects that experts in the discipline take seriously? In the past, I have worked with students to publish "biblical monologues" and dictionary articles; I have also included some students in research grants. Students learn best when they work alongside an expert.[19]

- *Consider what makes your college context unique and interesting.* Can you link this strength to your understanding or question? For example, your college might host an archive or rare book collection; it might have an excellent music, drama, or art department willing to collaborate; it might have successful alumni willing to help. Can you find a way to engage your students in these "real-world" learning opportunities?

- *Consider what your geographical context might offer, and link it to your understanding or question.* You might have access to a superb Holocaust museum, an exceptional sacred site, a funky cemetery, a traveling exhibit of the Dead Sea Scrolls, or a powerful memorial to the civil rights movement. Can you find a way to use these features to ground your students' learning in their immediate context?

With all of these factors in mind, decide on a summative assessment that will ask students to do something relevant, complex, and specific with the knowledge they acquire in order to generate understanding.

## Step 3. Identify Formative Assessments

If there are specific expectations of the type of product you expect, such as professional writing or presentation, try the following sample-template approach. If, on the other hand, you are open to students showing you they understand in any type of genre, then work with students to design their own formative development and assessments. They might choose to look at multiple samples and generate their own rubrics, for example. Because my context requires the specific development of expertise in "writing arguments," I use the sample-template approach. (My students find the sample template, which follows, to be one of the most effective tools they have ever had in learning how to write!)

Create a sample of the summative assessment you expect. As you work through it, note the knowledge you must use, the various skills you need to apply, the order of the steps you take, and the bottlenecks where you get stuck. Identify how you know when you are finished and have achieved success. In this way, you carefully think through what students will need to know and do in order to yield some level

---

19. See for example, S. P. Lajoie, "Transitions and Trajectories for Studies of Expertise," *Educational Researcher* 32, no. 8 (2003): 21–25.

of understanding. From the sample you create, devise a template of the form.[20] This will be the pattern of work you want to see replicated with different content. For example, with a short argument, the template asks the author to insert in the introduction the question in context, the thesis, and a preview of the main points that follow. The template requires each following paragraph to begin with a topic sentence that links the thesis and summarizes the evidence that follows, to include the evidence itself, and to conclude with a sentence that summarizes the evidence and sets up the next paragraph. The template shows that the final paragraph includes a review of the main points and thesis, and the implications for new contexts. As you become more aware of the cognitive decisions you make, you will have a better understanding of how to coach your students. Returning to your sample, add marginal notes (if you are working with a Word document, click "New Comment" under the Review tab) indicating how your sample and template align. This kind of metacognitive clarification takes the mystery out of the form, and frees the student to focus on understanding.

## Exhibit 3: Annotated Sample Template for Essay in "New Testament" (Webster)

Assignment #10

*Jane Webster*

Acts 1-12 describes the story of the early church from the ascension of Jesus to the time of Paul. On the one hand, Acts promotes unity and cooperation among the followers of Jesus; on the other hand, it identifies those in opposition to the church. In this way, Acts reflects discord between the early church and other groups at the time it was written.

Acts promotes unity and cooperation among the followers of Jesus. Acts refers to the followers of Jesus as a small group of Jews gathering

Identify the number of the assignment. This is the type of format and page layout required. Follow instructions about page length, cutting or adding detail as needed.

Identify the text that is the subject of study here. Treat the title of the book as the subject of most of your sentences.

This is preview #1

This is preview #2

Thesis

Extension Preview

Topic Sentence #1 (=preview #1) controls the content in this paragraph. Every sentence in the paragraph shows how Acts promotes unity and cooperation.

---

20. See Gerald Graff and Cathy Birkenstein, *"They Say /I Say": Moves That Matter in Academic Writing*, 3d ed (New York: Norton, 2014), for ideas on how to create writing templates.

together to pray (Acts 1:14; 2:1); it includes the named apostles, "certain women, including the mother of Jesus, and his brothers" (1:15). After the group receives the Holy Spirit (2:1-13), Peter makes a speech "standing with the eleven" to the "men of Judea and all who live in Jerusalem" (2:14). Peter aligns himself with his audience by calling them "descendants of David" (2:29). Many joined the group: first 3000 (2:41), then 5000 (4:4), then "day by day, the Lord added to their number" (2:47). This whole group were of "one heart and soul, and no one claimed private ownership of any possessions" (4:32; cf. 2:43). The apostles cured many of illnesses, adding to the number of the group (5:14-16). Those who had joined were held to a high standard (see 5:1-16; 6:1-6). As the story unfolds, the group began to include non-Jews: Samaritans (8:8, 14), a magician (8:13), an Ethiopian (8:39), and many Gentiles (10:44). Although the growing group of the followers of Jesus started among the Jews, many other people were welcomed into the group.

At the same time, the book of Acts identifies those who are in opposition to the church. For example, Peter states that even though the Israelites saw the works of Jesus, they "crucified" him (2:23; cf. 2:36; 3:15; 4:10); more specifically, he accuses "both Herod and Pontius Pilate, with

The first mention of a book should have the full name, but if there is no confusion, it does not need to be included again. Note how chapters are separated by a semi-colon.

See how you can paraphrase and summarize a bigger idea by selecting a few important words to put into quotation marks. Paraphrasing also helps to connect this reference to the topic sentence.

A range of verses in one chapter

Rather than providing details of the stories, just refer to them using the citations. Assume your reader can look them up. References to these stories is not intended to "retell" the sequence, but to use the stories as "evidence" in support of the topic sentence.

This is one chapter, but 2 separate verses.

This is the paragraph concluding sentence that reflects the same content of the topic sentence but perhaps adds more specifics.

Topic sentence #2 = preview #2

As you gather together ideas that you think will be good evidence to support your topic sentence, include examples as they occur to you, then edit carefully to link each sentence to the topic sentence and make the connections.

Note that I do not just "give a quote." I include the quoted material into a sentence that makes the connection between the quotation and my topic sentence.

the Gentiles and the peoples of Israel" (4:27; cf. 12:1). While some of these people repented and joined the believers, others challenged them. Twice "the priests, the captain of the temple, and the Sadducees" arrested some of the apostles (4:1; 5:17) and brought them before the rulers of the people and the elders (4:8; 5:27). When Stephen speaks in the temple, he calls the adversaries "stiff-necked people, uncircumcised in hearts and ears… forever opposing the Holy Spirit" and calls them "betrayers and murderers" (7:51-52). Saul of Tarsus approves of Stephen's murder (8:1) and persecutes the followers of Jesus, "ravaging the church by entering house after house; dragging off both men and women, he committed them to prison" (8:3). Herod executed James, the brother of Jesus (12:2). The book of Acts sets the members of the early church against the Jewish leaders because they killed Jesus and persecuted them.

Because Acts emphasizes the united but mixed group of believers and sets them over against the Jews, particularly the Jewish leaders, it reflects a time when the church was experiencing discord with other groups. This suggests a later date of authorship.

> I cited 4:27 but 12:1 refers to a similar example. I can include that example using "cf." which means "confer" or "compare to" or "see also." It is a handy way to include many references to the same sort of idea.

> Edit your paper by making your verbs strong so they "carry more weight" in your sentence. Revise passive verbs into active verbs. No "it is" or "there is."

> Concluding sentence reflects the same content as the topic sentence and adds specific content

> Preview #1

> Preview #2

> Thesis

> The extension is taken a little farther in the conclusion. In an essay that uses secondary sources, this will be the question to answer. What date do they assign to this text? Do scholars agree with this conclusion? What reasons do they provide?

Create a rubric. Rubrics usually take the form of grids that lay out what success looks like. You might try Rubistar or IRubric, but it is simple to create your own.

To check out Rubistar online rubrics builder go here:[21] .

For IRubric go here:[22]

Open a table (In MS Word, click "Insert Table" 5×5) to make formatting simpler. In the left column, list your criteria for grading, using such topics as content, organization, mechanics, research, citation, and so forth. Across the top row, identify your grading scale, usually from left to right from D to A. Starting with your B-column—what an average student at that level might achieve—begin to fill in your rubric with descriptors, eschewing vague adjectives such as "interesting" or "creative" for the more concrete verbs such as "includes," "describes," "connects," and "summarizes." Then move to the A-column to identify exemplary markers, and C- and D-columns to identify less satisfactory markers. Visually line up similar criteria, so students can easily see what they would need to do to move up to the next level. You can weigh each line differently if you like, to focus attention on one area or another. It is helpful to students if you use the same rubric for multiple assignments, if not all of them.[23] Alternatively, create space in the course for students to create their own template and rubric by comparing the features of multiple student samples.

When you have a summative assignment planned with its accompanying rubric, begin to map out the various skills that students will need to learn in order to do their project successfully. These are called "formative assessments" because they allow students to build necessary skills, but more importantly, they give you valuable information along the way about the student's understanding and skill level, and as a result, the opportunity to intervene with "just-in-time" teaching. Consider what your usual students are able to do at this particular level, and make a list of skills they need to succeed. For example, they may need to learn how to access data and archives, cite sources, read for argument, integrate the reasoning of others into

---

21. QR code URL: http://rubistar.4teachers.org/index.php.
22. QR code URL: http://www.rcampus.com/indexrubric.cfm.
23. See exhibit 4 in the appendix below for a sample rubric for writing assignments used across disciplines at Barton College.

their argument, insert a footnote, set up PowerPoint slides, find images online, or find a reference librarian. Some things to consider:

- Rank the knowledge and skills from foundational to more advanced.
- Include multiple opportunities to practice the same skills.
- With each subsequent learning opportunity, increase the grade weighting so students can "fail" in their first attempts but improve over time and still succeed in the course. Go from low-stakes assessment to high-stakes assessment.
- If at all possible, work within the same skill using different knowledge, or use the same knowledge and switch out the skill. This way, students only have to reformulate their understanding with one aspect at a time.

At this point in course design, I insert these skills sequentially into the master plan of the course, measured by classes, weeks, or units. I don't forget, however, that I will need to adjust the starting point and pace of the formative assessments based on the knowledge and skill of the actual students who show up in the course!

### Step 4. Create a Pre-Assessment

In order to measure learning at the end of the course, I like to know what students know when they first arrive in my course. I create a "pre-test" that I will give it to students as soon as they walk in the door. The pre-test will introduce students to content and ideas they will learn, will help them to realize that they might already know something but still have something interesting to learn, will give them a quiet opportunity to self-examine before they are "exposed to the other students and to me," and will break the awkwardness of the first class. I will have the opportunity to assess their knowledge level as a class and get a sense of how to pace the course. When the students finish the pre-test, I ask them if they were able to come up with some of the answers, if they were surprised by what they knew or didn't, and if they are interested in exploring the questions in more depth. Then, rather than work through the pre-test, we read through the syllabus together and students get a chance to see what they will learn in the course; right from the start, students "buy in" because their curiosity has been provoked. At the end of the semester, I return these pre-tests (ungraded). I ask them what they had said then, and what they would say now. They have usually forgotten how much they knew when they started the course and are pleasantly surprised that they have learned so much. It is also a good review of the larger themes of the course. (By the way, this is a great exercise to do just before you hand out student evaluations!)

In order to assess what students are able to do, I plan several skill-based, low-stakes "pre-assessments" early in the semester. I plan to meet students to review these assignments and to identify the "three strategies that will have the most impact on their grades" (they seem motivated by this language). While students gain some sense of control and responsibility for their own learning, I "distinguish between assessment *of* learning, [and] assessment *for* learning,"[24] by acquiring the baseline data I need to adjust the pace and to focus instruction.[25]

## Step 5: Mapping Out the Plan

Once I have decided on the summative assessment and determined the necessary order of the formative assessments, I begin to slot the assessments into the course calendar, taking into consideration other events in the semester—such as the deadline to drop, semester breaks, and long weekends—in order not to exasperate students or to overload them unnecessarily. I also consider my own workload schedule, so that I have time to provide prompt feedback to students, preferably by the next class meeting. I try to pace the workload evenly throughout the semester, often lightening the load toward the end; I find that students develop good work habits and adjust more readily to consistent workload expectations than to fewer, more spaced-out demands. Finally, I work some flexibility into the schedule for students by dropping the lowest assignment grades or by giving a choice of assignments at the end of the semester. This way, if students have emergencies, they have a built-in contingency plan; they also have more opportunities to experiment for low stakes. I also know I must adjust the pace of the course to accommodate students' skills and knowledge.

Up to this point, these design elements will work for any course.

## Step 6: Insert the Knowledge

After I map out the design for skill development, I begin to insert the biblical-studies content. I select various objects of study—such as texts, films, or art—that contribute different ideas to the formation of the enduring understanding or address the metaquestion. I arrange these in a relatively logical order, and slot them into the course matrix.

At this point, my course structure is well planned: the enduring understanding or metaquestion gives it focus, and opportunities for students to learn the knowledge and skills to arrive at this understanding are in place. Having described my design process—hopefully, in such a way that I might provoke the same questions for you as you design your own—I will describe in more detail the decisions and rationale I have made in the design of my "Introduction to the New Testament" course.

---

24. Carol Ann Tomlinson, "Learning to Love Assessment," *Educational Leadership* 65, no. 4 (2007): 13.
25. Carol Oberg, "Guiding Classroom Instruction through Performance Assessment," *Journal of Case Studies in Accreditation and Assessment* 1 (2010): 1–11.

## Putting Understanding by Design to Work: Introduction to New Testament

### The Metaquestion

Although I have experimented with different metaquestions in my religious-studies courses, the one that works the best in my New Testament course is "What is truth?" The question addresses the cognitive challenges of emerging adults to determine who and what will have authority in their lives and why. It also provokes critical thinking and writing skills; as students construct their own arguments, they need to evaluate the truth-claims of the biblical text, their own truth-claims in selecting and ordering the evidence, and the truth-claims of biblical scholars. The question arises spontaneously in class discussion when students explore competing observations (Did Jesus die on Passover or the day before?), theories (Is Q the Gospel of Thomas?), and experiences (How is someone saved?). And because we are not pinning truth down to one specific "enduring understanding," students are free to meet the question where they are and to construct their own understanding. While in some of my courses the metaquestion serves as the focus of the summative assessment, in this course I use the metaquestion more as a framing device, which I will explain more fully below.

### Writing to Learn; Learning to Write

At Barton College, I offer New Testament to all students as a general education global-awareness course with a writing-intensive focusing on how to write a short argument. To conform to college requirements, I require students to conduct research, to cite sources appropriately, to write at least twenty pages graded with an institutional rubric, and to complete at least one assignment with guided revision. I must also teach our religion majors how to write within the discipline of religious studies.

I use this curriculum requirement to get "buy-in" from the students, but I also provide statistics from employers stating that the ability to write an argument is one of the most important job skills. I will teach them to use a template that they will use for most reports, executive summaries, and job applications; they will use the same basic form for essays in their other courses. They will learn to self- and peer-assess. They will get repeated practice using different content, so they will become very proficient with the argument form.

I have found that as I teach them how to write using this template, I am also able to teach them how to think in a systematic and productive way. I spend a great deal of time—both in class and out—describing how to read a section of the New Testament (e.g., all of Mark), to identify themes or patterns, to gather evidence, to compile sentences, and to evaluate and cite sources. I show students how to interpret their evidence by gathering it into paragraphs and framing it with topic and concluding sentences. When they set this paragraph beside another, similar paragraph, they will notice a larger pattern, such as what the author might be promoting.[26] (This is their thesis.) They must then consider why the author might promote this idea: Is there something happening in the social or historical context provoking the writing of this text? (We call this the extension, but it corresponds to "explanation" and/or "interpretation.") When students realize that they will learn the valuable job skills of critical thinking and generating arguments, they invest time and effort into these formative assignments.

After students have written three low-stakes assignments to demonstrate their ability to write (a self-reflective paragraph on their view of the authority of the Bible, a paragraph describing how biblical scholars define the "gospel genre," and their first essay on Mark), I review the papers with students to outline a plan for improvement: we might work at the word level (aim for accurate and precise vocabulary), sentence level (subordinate and main clauses, active verbs, transitions, citations), paragraph level (topic and concluding sentences), introduction and conclusion (thesis, extension, relevance, metaquestion). We might work on selecting and citing sources, paraphrasing, or bibliography format. I encourage students to help each other to develop these skills. In this way, I get to know the students, build some trust, teach specific skills, and set realistic development goals. I give them feedback on their progress at midterm and final, sometimes revising the goals.

As students learn to write, they also develop their understanding by putting their knowledge to work. Throughout the semester, they write sixteen one- to two-page arguments, building an argument for or against various prompts or in response to questions. For example, in the first half of the course, students find their own voice by writing a series of papers on the Christology and/or soteriology of each Gospel based solely on primary sources. Starting at midterm, students continue to make their own conclusions, but then compare their conclusions to scholarly opinions: they learn to conduct research, to evaluate the scholars' use of evidence, bias, and perspective, and to integrate these opinions into their arguments. I prompt these later essays with questions such as this: What is the value of the Gospel of Thomas for historical-Jesus research? How dependable is the Acts of the Apostles for the historical Paul? So, while students are learning how to write short arguments (using a template and rubric), they also develop surface cultural literacy (names of characters, events, etc.), awareness of deeper structures of ancient culture (authority, power, rhetoric, agenda, bias, etc.), and an understanding of the impact of this ancient culture on contemporary society.

I use the rubric in exhibit 5 (see the appendix, below) to assess their work. Note that it uses much of the same language as the cross-disciplinary institutional rubric (exhibit 4), but that it includes a number of discipline-specific features and breaks down the writing process into two stages: writing an argument based on primary sources alone and writing an argument that engages the scholarship. When students use the same rubric through different assignments, they develop confidence in the form and use the form to get leverage into understanding.

---

26. I find that when I use the word *promoting* and connect it to contemporary advertising, students can more readily step outside the narrative and see the agenda and bias of the text.

I also use the writing assignments to bring my own background, scholarship, and interests into the course design. I entered biblical studies in order to explore the role of women in relationship to the divine and in the contemporary church, so I am both comfortable and interested in working with feminist hermeneutics. I am also the only female faculty member who teaches in the Religion and Philosophy program. I can therefore take advantage of my unique presence in this context to raise important questions about feminist biblical interpretation and about women in churches and the workplace. Because of this, I integrate into the latter half of my New Testament course a three-tiered exploration of the role of women in the early church. First, students write a one-page argument about Paul's attitude toward women in ministry according to 1 Corinthians, Romans 16, and Galatians 3:28-29; then, they write a one-page argument based on 1 Timothy, framed by their conclusion from the previous essay; finally, they write an argument based on the Acts of Paul and Thecla, comparing it to 1 Corinthians and 1 Timothy. They frame this last argument with secondary-source arguments about why the Acts of Paul and Thecla is not included in the New Testament canon. (As the summative writing assessment, this two-page essay receives a heftier grade.) On the day these essays are due, I aim for the "enduring understanding" that the New Testament is neither silent nor single-minded about the role of women in the church, despite what many religious authorities claim. I tap into the students' own stories and questions of sexuality, gender confusion, inequality, violence, racism, oppression, and conflict. I can raise metaquestions about the source and nature of truth and authority, and explore with students their own developing autonomy and identity. In this way, I align the course questions, the students' questions, and my own questions for fruitful dialogue.

Once students have invested significant time and energy into crafting their arguments based on the NT texts, they are better prepared to engage in class discussions. We do not need to linger on the specifics, but can put knowledge to use directly. I usually start each class with a particular question: What did you think about this text? How is it similar or different to others we have explored? What does this text emphasize about Jesus? What do you think is happening in the community that prompted this text? What are the clues? What piece does this text contribute to the overall understanding of Jesus and/or Christianity? Which one has greater authority or is more "true"? One of these questions will generally spark a lively discussion and we just go wherever it leads us, often into the differences between religious, social, ethical, or political positions. Students thus have the opportunity to examine personal identity and meaning when and as they are so inclined, to consider the larger metaquestion about truth and authority, and to develop their ability to speak about these topics with curiosity and respect.

Constrained by the general education goals to develop written communication, and religion-major goals to develop writing and knowledge in the discipline, and taking into account the students' own goals of spiritual quest, I therefore design a summative assessment of their writing that includes both primary and secondary research and addresses a question relevant for our particular and unique context.

## Biblical Literacy

As a course in the general education "global-awareness basket," my "Introduction to the New Testament" course must demonstrate that students understand how the Bible both shapes Western culture and, in turn, how its interpretation is shaped by culture. Because we are located in rural North Carolina in the "heart of the Bible Belt," most students are familiar with the general themes of the Bible, but they have seldom read much of it themselves. Some approach the Bible as the direct word of God, rendering it both infallible and authoritative. Some are familiar with the church year and holidays. Very few of them, according to the pre-test, are able to answer basic questions such as when the New Testament was written, by whom, in what language, in what geographical location or political environment; few can list more than four characters (Jesus, Mary, Joseph, and Judas), more than five NT books (four Gospels and Revelation), or more than one way that a person "can be saved" ("By believing Jesus is my Lord and Savior"). Most claim to know the book of Revelation better than any other book, although what they know is rarely accurate. Because students have an overconfident view of their own knowledge, and because the Bible is often used (poorly) in ethical debate, I set as the goal the following enduring understanding: "Biblical literacy contributes to cultural awareness."

I struggled for a long time to find a way to assess student knowledge without feeling obliged to "cover content" in the classroom—I wanted to create space for discussions about metaquestions and personal meaning and identity. If I gave students reading quizzes, they seemed only to develop their memorization skills. A few years ago, I set up a series of online "biblical-literacy" quizzes (standard basic knowledge found in most NT textbooks) that students could take as many times as they wanted; they would receive feedback but their grades would not count. (Some textbook publishers offer these sorts of online quizzes.) I urge students to take these tests before they do the reading for the unit, before the unit class, after the class, every day until they have mastered the content, and then to review for tests.[27] I encourage students to ask or research anything they do not understand. In this way, I found that I am relieved of "delivering content": more importantly, students are less anxious about how and what to know and can concentrate on using the knowledge they learn to develop their writing skills and enduring understanding.

This enduring understanding—that biblical literacy contributes to cultural awareness—influences my decisions about how to select and to order the content. Because I hope that students will understand the arc of the New Testament narrative and how it affects culture (such as how we organize social life around Christmas and Easter), I opt to set up the course content in canonical order.[28]

---

27. See Peter C. Brown, Henry L. Roediger III, and Mark A. McDaniel, *Make It Stick: The Science of Successful Learning* (Cambridge: Harvard University Press, 2014), for the value of repeated memory retrieval.

28. Other biblical-studies teachers select and order different texts to address their enduring understanding. For example, if their big idea focused on Jesus' ethics, they might just read the Sermon on the Mount; if their big idea focused on Paul's creation of Christianity, they might just read Paul's letters; if

In order to expose students to the multitude of NT voices, and hence divergent cultural manifestations (e.g., understandings of the human condition, ethics, and church polity), I invite them to read and write about major sections from most of the NT books before class; they come to class already familiar with the content, so we devote the class time to questions and to exploring possible explanations for the differences, such as the four-source theory of the Gospels or theories on the authorship of the Pauline letters. For this reason, I opt not to use a textbook: students have the opportunity to create their own understanding from the knowledge they have gathered and analyzed themselves through writing.[29] Thus, I select and order the content in order to serve the goal of the targeted enduring understanding that biblical literacy cultivates cultural awareness.

I measure what I want students to know—biblical literacy—and what I want students to do—write competently—with a summative-assessment final exam (which follows the same format as a lower-stakes midterm exam). I give students multiple-choice questions that test their recognition of major figures and events of the New Testament as well as some of the major scholarly theories of authorship, date, composition, genre, canonization, and purpose of the various NT books. I also require students to write well-constructed comparative essays—graded with a familiar rubric—that assess their understanding of the content, their ability to write short arguments, and their engagement with the metaquestion. At midterm, I ask students to compare the Gospel traditions, using this essay question:

> Explain why Matthew and Luke rewrote the Gospel of Mark. What did each find troubling or missing and how did they fill the gaps to present Jesus in a new way? What sociohistorical context might have influenced their choices? Frame your essay with a discussion of why there are four Gospels in the New Testament, and why knowing this helps us to understand our culture.

On their final exam, they write two essays:

1. *"Several historical events have influenced the shape of the New Testament canon."* Briefly describe two of these events, what NT texts were written or canonized in response, and explain why. Frame your essay with a discussion of why it is important to consider historical context (both then and now) when interpreting the New Testament, and why knowing this helps us to understand our culture.

2. *"It is important to distinguish the difference between what Paul says himself, what others say in his name, and what others say about him."* Argue for or against this thesis statement, clearly distinguishing which NT texts fall into which category. Frame this argument with a discussion

---

their big idea aims to identify biblical motifs in popular culture, they might read only enough of the NT to provide the background for interpreting film, literature, art, music, media, and politics.

29. I do put a number of excellent textbooks on reserve in the library as resources.

about "What is truth?" and why knowing this helps us to understand our culture.

Because the writing demands are so high in this course and require students to use information from the New Testament, I opt to keep the assessment of biblical literacy at a relatively low cognitive level.

### Personal Identity and Meaning

Although I think it is important for students to have the opportunity to explore their personal sense of identity, meaning, and purpose, I do not measure their learning with any formal assessment in this course. However, I do provide multiple opportunities for students to reflect on the questions throughout the course. For example, on the pre-test, I ask them how they would describe their relationship with the Bible. In class, I invite them to give examples of their own experience with religious rituals and understanding. (Would anyone like to share an example of a time when you observed a baptism? How have you heard people talk about "being saved"?) I invite them to add comments or questions to their written assignments or exams: How has your relationship with the Bible stayed the same or changed throughout this course? How do you account for the differences? What is your response to the Timothy's silencing of women? I invite them to speak to me privately or to ask questions in class. I therefore give students many opportunities to explore these questions of spiritual quest—and the metaquestion, "What is truth?"—in personal ways that do not have an impact on their evaluation.

## Conclusion

In sum, these are the decisions I have made that have had the most leverage on student understanding. First, I awaken cross-disciplinary curiosity and spiritual and cognitive development with a metaquestion: in this case, "What is truth?" Second, I help students grapple with an enduring understanding that fits the institutional, curricular, program, and personal needs of the context: biblical literacy cultivates cultural awareness. Third, I help students learn the knowledge they need to construct their own understanding by exposing them to a wide variety of biblical texts. And fourth, I help students to develop the skills they will need to show me they understand, in this case, how to construct and write an argument. Finally, I make space in the classroom for students to explore personal meaning through reflecting on the "truth" of the Bible for them. Understanding by Design has provided me with an extremely useful matrix to design thoughtful, fair, relevant, and well-structured learning opportunities for my students that lead to understanding important ideas by developing knowledge and skills.

## Works Cited

Astin, Alexander, Helen Astin, and Jennifer Lindholm. *Cultivating the Spirit: How College Can Enhance Students' Inner Lives.* San Francisco: Jossey-Bass, 2011.

Berlinerblau, Jacques. *The Secular Bible: Why Non-believers Must Take Religion Seriously*. New York: Cambridge University Press, 2005.

Brown, Peter C., Henry L. Roediger III, and Mark A. McDaniel. *Make It Stick: The Science of Successful Learning*. Cambridge: Harvard University Press, 2014.

Chickering, Arthur W., and Associates, *The Modern American College: Responding to the New Realities of Diverse Students and a Changing Society*. San Francisco: Jossey-Bass, 1981.

Davidovitch, Nitza. "Learning-Centered Teaching and Backward Course Design: From Transferring Knowledge To Teaching Skills." *Journal of International Education Research* 9, no. 4 (2013): 329–38.

Dyas, Dee, and Esther Hughes. *The Bible in Western Culture: The Student's Guide*. New York: Routledge, 2005.

Graff, Gerald, and Cathy Birkenstein. *"They Say /I Say": Moves That Matter in Academic Writing*. 3d ed. New York: Norton, 2014.

Lajoie, S. P. "Transitions and Trajectories for Studies of Expertise." *Educational Researcher* 32. no. 8 (2003): 21–25.

Lampert, Magdalene. *Teaching Problems and the Problems of Teaching*. New Haven: Yale University Press, 2001.

Love, Patrick G., and Victoria L. Guthrie. *Understanding and Applying Cognitive Development Theory: New Directions for Student Services*. San Francisco: Jossey-Bass, 1999.

Oberg, Carol. "Guiding Classroom Instruction through Performance Assessment." *Journal of Case Studies in Accreditation and Assessment* 1 (2010): 1–11.

Parks, Sharon Daloz. *Big Questions, Worthy Dreams: Mentoring Emerging Adults in Their Search for Meaning, Purpose, and Faith*. San Francisco: Jossey-Bass, 2000.

Perry, William G., Jr. *Forms of Intellectual and Ethical Development in the College Years—A Scheme*. New York: Holt, Rinehart and Winston 1968, 1970.

Poe, Marshall. "Colleges Should Teach Religion to Their Students: When students feel adrift, spiritual guidance might help." http://www.theatlantic.com/education/archive/2014/03/colleges-should-teach-religion-to-their-students/284296.

Prothero, Stephen. *Religious Literacy: What Every American Needs to Know about Religion—and Doesn't*. New York: HarperCollins, 2007.

Roncase, Mark, and Patrick Gray, eds. *Teaching the Bible: Practical Strategies for Classroom Instruction*. Atlanta: Society of Biblical Literature, 2005.

———. *Teaching the Bible through Popular Culture and the Arts*. Atlanta: Society of Biblical Literature, 2007.

Schippe, Cullen, and Chuck Stetson, eds. *The Bible and Its Influence*. New York: Bible Literacy Project, 2006.

Tomlinson, Carol Ann. "Learning to Love Assessment." *Educational Leadership* 65, no. 4 (2007): 8–13.

Walvoord, Barbara E. *Teaching and Learning in the College Introductory Religion Courses*. Malden, MA: Wiley-Blackwell, 2008.

Webster, Jane S., and Glenn S. Holland, eds. *Teaching the Bible in the Liberal Arts Classroom*. Sheffield, UK: Sheffield Phoenix, 2012.

———, James J. Buckley, Tim Jensen, and Stacey Floyd-Thomas. "Responses to the AAR-Teagle White Paper: 'The Religious Studies Major in a Post-9/11 World.'" *Teaching Theology & Religion* 14, no. 1 (January 2011): 34–71.

Weimer, Maryellen. *Learner-Centered Teaching: Five Key Changes to Practice*. San Francisco: Jossey-Bass, 2002.

Wray, T. J.. *What the Bible Really Tells Us: The Essentials Guide to Biblical Literacy*. New York: Rowman and Littlefield, 2011.

## Web sites

Bible Literacy Project: http://www.bibleliteracy.org/Site/index.htm

Commission on the Humanities and Social Sciences, American Academy of Arts and Sciences, "The Heart of the Matter": http://www.humanitiescommission.org/_pdf/hss_report.pdf.

Society for Biblical Literature, "Teaching the Bible": http://www.sbl-site.org/educational/teachingbible.aspx

Association of American Colleges and Universities, "Top Ten Things Employers Look for in New Graduates": http://www.aacu.org/leap/students/employerstopten.cfm.

James Madison University, "William Perry's Scheme Of Intellectual And Ethical Development": http://www.jmu.edu/geology/evolutionarysystems/protected/handouts/willperry2.pdf.

A Teacher's Guide to Religion in the Public Schools (085.10-FAC) http://www.firstamendmentcenter.org/publications.

# Chapter 6

# Teaching Outside of the Bible with Understanding by Design

*Christopher M. Jones*

I am a biblical scholar by training. My PhD is in Hebrew Bible and my dissertation analyzes space, identity, and power in Ezra-Nehemiah. At the time that I am writing this chapter, I am completing the first semester of my first academic appointment, as visiting assistant professor of religious studies at Beloit College. The position is something of a dream job: I teach two courses per semester at a small liberal-arts college, and I have near-total carte blanche to teach whatever I want to teach within the disciplines of religious studies and Jewish studies. The only catch? Because my department already has a biblical scholar on staff, they do not need for me to offer any biblical-studies courses. I am a biblical scholar who teaches, quite literally, anything but Bible.

It may seem peculiar that a book entitled *Understanding Bible by Design* would include a chapter on using Understanding by Design (hereafter, UbD) for courses outside of biblical studies. It shouldn't be. In today's academic job market, the ability to teach practically anything, in practically any setting, is a survival skill. The academic labor market is glutted with eminently qualified candidates in search of a dwindling number of full-time appointments. Colleges and universities face rising tuitions and steep budget cutbacks. Higher education is expected to prepare students for an increasingly specialized and competitive job market. As academic job seekers, we need to be flexible in our teaching competencies, and we need to be able to maintain a robust research schedule while we teach courses on a wide variety of topics. The rule is no longer publish or perish. The rule is publish or be stillborn.

---

*https://beloit.academia.edu/ChristopherJones

If you have never used UbD, and you're reading this book because you're curious about what it's like to learn UbD from the ground up while using it to design new courses, then this chapter will be particularly interesting to you. Unlike the other two authors in this volume, I had no prior experience with UbD before I used it to design two new courses in my first academic appointment—in fact, I'd never even heard of it. In this chapter, I relate my experience of using it for the first time. First, I assess how difficult it was for me to learn the UbD framework. Then, I delve into the details of how I used it in practice. In the process, I relate both my successes and my failures, since both will be instructive to you as you consider whether to adopt UbD in your own teaching praxis. My thesis is simple: *UbD works*. It is not prohibitively difficult to learn, and it can be learned on the fly, while you design your courses. It will make your courses better, even if you only partially implement it in your design process. I strongly encourage anybody who is serious about improving their pedagogical practice to try UbD.

## Understanding by Design as Method and as Framework

I turned to UbD, not because I wanted to experiment with a fresh approach to course design, but because I needed to streamline the whole design process. It was my first semester as a full-time instructor, and I was teaching two courses outside of my field of expertise. I was also slated to defend my dissertation during the semester. I looked to UbD as a sensible way to contain and focus the work of designing a course. Grant Wiggins and Jay McTighe caution that some educators find UbD to be "a bit awkward and time-consuming until you get the hang of it,"[1] but I have found the opposite to be true. Because UbD ties both content and assessment to departmental and institutional directives, it helps to focus the process of course design. Moreover, because UbD unites course content, in the design phase, around a discrete set of central ideas, UbD also might streamline preparation time for individual class sessions. Ideally, each session has already been designed to fit into a broader conceptual matrix; thus, the one-time intellectual work of establishing that matrix during the design phase pays exponential dividends during the semester: each class session builds on the previous sessions along a preestablished conceptual framework.

I have also found that UbD is better for our students. Most of us learned to teach by delivering content in a survey format, using the "coverage" model, and we learned to tie assessment to whatever we managed to cover. Assessment, in this model, ends up testing what we think we told our students; it does not necessarily test what they learned. UbD, by contrast, advocates that we tie both content and assessment to a set of established goals, and that we design the assessments *before* we determine the content. Because the course, as a whole, is held together by a small set of essential questions, students have a sense of how things fit together, and they know, from the start, what sorts of understandings they will be called

---

1. Grant P. Wiggins and Jay McTighe, *Understanding by Design*, exp. 2d ed. (Alexandria, VA: Association for Supervision and Curriculum Development, 2005), 21.

upon to demonstrate during their assessments. By emphasizing coherent, purposeful design, UbD enhances student agency, and it shifts the intellectual burden of preparing students for assessments from the professor to the student.[2]

Now that I have finished teaching the courses, it is tempting to use this chapter to describe the courses as I wish I'd designed and taught them, but that would subvert the spirit of this book. Instead, I'll describe what I actually did, mistakes included. Both my successes and my failures tell the same story: *UbD works*. The biggest mistake I made, in retrospect, is that I did not commit more fully to the UbD model. The most successful moments in both courses came as a result of the sort of high-level integration that UbD facilitates. The weakest elements in both courses, meanwhile, were those that I had included on the basis of the "coverage" model,[3] without tying them explicitly to a set of bigger ideas. If anything, the UbD model conditioned my students to expect each class session not only to build on previous sessions but to call past learning into question; when they sensed that they were being taught something just because I thought they should know about it, they lost interest. *This is a good thing*. It reflects the fact that UbD made my students active participants in their own learning, rather than passive recipients of knowledge that I dispensed.[4]

The fundamental, underlying argument made by the UbD template is that students only internalize big, counterintuitive ideas if they encounter those ideas repeatedly, in different forms, over the course of a well-planned semester. I found that this held true as well for the UbD model itself. I committed to using UbD from the very start of my course planning for the spring of 2014. I treated UbD like a step-by-step process for course design: I identified big ideas, enduring understandings, and essential questions; then I designed assessments; finally, I sketched out daily reading assignments. Having designed the courses, I put UbD aside once the semester started.

In retrospect, I misunderstood UbD as a prescriptive course-design methodology, when in fact it is something much more ambitious: it is a conceptual framework, a way of imagining the entire teaching process, from scheduling readings to writing assessments to creating daily lesson plans. Like any conceptual framework, its cognitive integration takes time. Although I had read *Understanding by Design* before I started designing my two courses for the spring of 2014, in retrospect I don't think I'd yet fully internalized UbD on a conceptual level. Rather, throughout

---

2. It should not be lost on teachers of religion that Jonathan Z. Smith also advocates backward course design, albeit not within the UbD framework. Smith says that crafting a syllabus should start at the end, with the issues that will be covered in the final examination. Each session, then, should be part of a road map designed to lead to the destination articulated by the final. See Jonathan Z. Smith, "Introduction: Approaching the College Classroom," in *On Teaching Religion*, ed. Christopher I. Lehrich (New York: Oxford University Press, 2013), 1–8, esp. 2–3. For a critical reassessment of Smith's pedagogy, see Kathryn Lofton, review of Jonathan Z. Smith and Christopher I. Lehrich, *On Teaching Religion*, in *Journal of the American Academy of Religion* 82 (2014): 531–42 (hereafter *JAAR*).

3. See esp. Wiggins and McTighe, *Understanding by Design*, 17–18.

4. The distinction between active engagement and passive absorption, meanwhile, invokes Paolo Freire's rejection of the "banking" model; see, idem, *Pedagogy of the Oppressed*, trans. Myra Bergman Ramos (New York: Continuum, 1993), 52–105.

the semester, UbD continued to operate alongside of the "coverage" model that I had acquired in my graduate-school training. The result was an odd mish-mash: I designed the courses themselves on the basis of the UbD framework, but I scheduled individual class sessions by simply assigning readings from the textbooks that covered relevant material, and I prepared for each class session without paying sufficient attention to how it fit into the broader design. I also provided assessments that did not build on one another, which discouraged students from seeking larger-scale syntheses of course content. Looking back, that seems like it should have been obvious that this was the wrong approach, yet at the time it wasn't. Big ideas (UbD included) integrate themselves slowly into our minds, especially when they come up against other deeply entrenched prior conceptions.

In the next section, I will lay out the institutional and departmental context in which I taught those courses, since that helped me to determine the overarching goals for each course. One of the most useful aspects of UbD is the way that it encourages teachers to tie course objectives to institutional objectives.[5] Stage 1 of the UbD template is to "Identify Desired Results," and the first step in that process is to identify, in turn, a set of "Established Goals."[6] These goals are determined, at least in part, by an entity external to the course itself; for most teachers employed in higher education, this entity will be the institution or the department. Initiating course design with respect to external standards has two immediate and enduring benefits. First, it saves time. We begin course planning not with the "terror of a blank page,"[7] but, rather, with a set of institutional objectives that limit the horizon of possibilities without foreclosing them entirely. Second, it builds the work of integration into the course-planning process. If every course is designed around a set of "big ideas" that are drawn, in turn, from a set of publicly stated departmental and institutional objectives, then some level of integration between our course offerings and those of our colleagues is built into the course-design process. UbD frees us to devote the first fruits of our energies to the course at hand, without fretting overmuch about how that course will relate to the broader institutional matrix.

## My Context: Beloit College

Beloit College is a small, private, residential liberal-arts college located in the town of Beloit, Wisconsin. The institution furnishes several discrete institutional objectives by its very nature as a small liberal-arts college. There is an emphasis on critical thinking, on high-level literacy, and on broad exposure to a variety of academic disciplines. Beloit College further distinguishes itself within its cohort of peer institutions in at least three ways. First, there is a pervasive emphasis on student agency—students have considerable freedom to design their own academic programs, and they are expected to contribute actively to their learning in their coursework. Second, the college sees itself as a hub between the local and the

---

5. Wiggins and McTighe, *Understanding by Design*, 18, et passim.
6. Ibid., 56–81.
7. Smith, "Approaching the College Classroom," 2.

global, in which students become aware of their own positionality with respect to the world around them. Finally, in response to the old canard that the liberal arts are impractical, Beloit College has a Liberal Arts in Practice requirement, and a campus center devoted to assisting students in fulfilling it.

Though Beloit College, in its early history, was informally associated with the Congregationalist tradition, it is now religiously unaffiliated—in fact, Beloit College has a reputation for being among the most secular colleges in the United States. It also has a robust and vital religious-studies program, and its religious-studies courses attract both religious and nonreligious students. The Department of Philosophy and Religious Studies has its own distinctive emphases that it uses to structure the educational experiences of religious-studies majors and minors. We aim to reinforce to our students that all religious practices, regardless of the broader influences across time and space that may partially determine them, are only intelligible as eminently *local* phenomena, fully embedded in their immediate contexts. Because context is always multifaceted, we conceptualize religious studies as innately interdisciplinary, requiring broad competencies drawn from sociology, anthropology, history, geography, and literary studies. The ultimate goal of religious-studies courses is the development of a critical awareness of one's own cultural situatedness in relation to other people.

---

 Check out the "Religious Studies" program of Beloit College.[8]

---

These broad departmental and institutional emphases provide a basis for identifying established goals in Stage 1 of the UbD template. The three goals on which I have chosen to focus, based on the distinctive emphases outlined by my institution and my department, are interdisciplinarity, cultural competency, and awareness of the relationship between the local and the global. The next "step" in the UbD template is to identify the enduring understandings that students must acquire to meet these goals; such understandings, in turn, depend upon the acquisition of knowledge and the mastery of skill sets. Wiggins and McTighe encourage teachers to tie these objectives together around a set of core "big ideas."[9] There are various ways to dissect this part of the process, so I chose to begin with big ideas and work backwards to enduring understandings. The big ideas, I found, arose naturally out of the interaction between my established goals and the potential content of each individual course. The remainder of the UbD framework, meanwhile, is tied to these big ideas: these ideas are the source of the essential questions and the enduring understandings that tie a course together, and the other aspects of the course

---

8. QR code URL: http://www.beloit.edu/religious/.
9. Wiggins and McTighe, *Understanding by Design*, 34, 56–60.

(i.e., assessments and actual learning experiences) are designed to produce understandings that are linked, in turn, to these essential questions.

In the remainder of this chapter, I will demonstrate how I used the institutional and departmental goals laid out for me in my distinct pedagogical context to generate unifying conceptual frameworks for two courses that I taught at Beloit College in the spring of 2014: "Ritual and Ritualization" and "Space and Place in Early Judaism." I will discuss each course in turn, describing (1) how I drew core ideas out of the interaction between institutional goals and the distinct subject area covered in the class; (2) how I used those core ideas to generate essential questions; (3) how I used those essential questions, in turn, to generate enduring understandings; (4) how I used enduring understandings to design assessments; and, (5) finally, how I designed individual lessons with respect to those assessments. At the conclusion of the chapter, I will reflect briefly on how each course worked in practice and what I would do differently in the future.

## Course #1: "Ritual and Ritualization"

### Big Ideas

I structured my course on ritual studies around two core ideas: *reification* and *practice*. Reification is, literally and etymologically, *thing*-ifying: it is the process of transforming an abstraction into something concrete. For example, people have been making visual representations of their own faces for untold millennia, and self-portraiture became a distinctive artistic genre during the early European Renaissance. The first photographic self-portrait was taken in 1839, and it was not uncommon for people to take their own portraits in the mirror throughout the twentieth century.[10] With the advent of the Internet, photographic self-portraits quickly made their way online. Yet the "selfie" did not become a recognizable cultural phenomenon until 2012.[11] By 2013, it was the Oxford Dictionaries Word of the Year,[12] and it is now part of common English vernacular. The emergence of the term *selfie* as a catch-all for self-portraits taken specifically to be posted online has, in turn, lent definition to the phenomenon itself. There is now a grammar of sorts for it: depending on things like posture, clothing, and camera angle, selfies can connote sexual confidence, ironic detachment, or simple narcissism. The selfie is now a thing.

The analytical category *ritual* is, *par excellence*, an example of scholarly reification. Not all languages have a term for ritual, and those that do connote a wide variety of different related phenomena with their respective nomenclatures. In

---

10. "Selfie," Wikipedia, http://en.wikipedia.org/wiki/Selfie.
11. "Top Ten Everything of 2012," *Time*, http://newsfeed.time.com/2012/12/04/top-10-news-lists/slide/selfie/. The *Oxford English Dictionary* finds the first attestation of the term "selfie" on an Australian Internet message board in 2002, and it cites examples from throughout the first decade of the twenty-first century; see "Selfie," in *OED*, 3d ed. (Oxford: Oxford University Press, 2014). However, the term was largely unknown except in certain online subcultures until the last few years.
12. "The Oxford Dictionaries Word of the Year is . . . ," http://blog.oxforddictionaries.com/2013/11/word-of-the-year-2013-winner/.

Western academia, however, the term *ritual*, as an analytical category, always arrives with a load of Protestant, Eurocentric bias.[13] From the outset, it was commonly used in Protestant circles to connote empty formalism in contradistinction to inner substance.[14] When the term first entered scholarly discourse, in the late nineteenth century, ritual was what "primitive" peoples did, in contrast with normal practice in the modern West. The term, moreover, came to signify for scholars the universality of their modern perspective, in contrast with the myopic particularism of indigenous practices.[15] When we call something ritual, we assert that it is like other things that we call ritual, and we imply that we, as scholars, have a universal and objective perspective for making that connection.[16]

In providing all of this disciplinary history, I wanted to reinforce to my students that we do not simply encounter ritual in the world; rather, when we refer to practices that have ritual-like characteristics (e.g., formality, invariance, traditionalism, rule governance, performativity, sanctity[17]) as ritual, we are importing an interpretive history teeming with biased misrepresentation. Moreover, because we, as Westerners, sit at the apex of the world's power structures, we impose a hegemonic discourse on non-Western peoples simply through the act of labeling. This is a legitimate problem, one for which I have no definitive solution. If we refrain entirely from labeling, we lose a powerful analytical category. If, on the other hand, we use ritual as an analytical category, we imply that it is a universal, substantive phenomenon; in so doing, we risk ignoring (and therefore suppressing) what is distinctive about a particular cluster of practices in its embedded context.

By organizing the course around the idea of reification, I wanted to foreground this problem for my students, for two reasons. First, it is an essential concept in contemporary ritual theory. Second, however, it also supports all three of my departmental goals (interdisciplinarity, cultural competency, and local/global awareness). By emphasizing to students the reification of the category *ritual*, I wanted to reinforce to them, on a conceptual level, that academic disciplines use different abstract categories to carve up the world, so what students learn in their college classes always comes to them through a disciplinary filter. Reification is also a means to teach cultural competency and global/local awareness: theoretical abstractions, by subsuming discrete human practices into universal frameworks, only make them intelligible to outside observers at the cost of their unique particularity. Students need to know that scholars use the term *ritual* because it is useful, not because it is inevitable. There are other ways to understand formalized, rule-governed, invariant, symbolically dense human actions.

---

13. Talal Asad, *Genealogies of Religion: Discipline and Reasons of Power in Christianity and Islam* (Baltimore: Johns Hopkins University Press, 1993), 56–57.

14. Jonathan Z. Smith, *To Take Place: Toward Theory in Ritual*, Chicago Studies in the History of Judaism (Chicago: University of Chicago Press, 1987), 96–102.

15. Catherine Bell, *Ritual: Perspectives and Dimensions* (Oxford: Oxford University Press, 1997), 259–62.

16. Ibid., 262; Catherine Bell, *Ritual Theory, Ritual Practice* (New York: Oxford University Press, 1992), 47–54.

17. Ibid., 138–69.

The problem of reification also provides the point of connection to the course's other core idea: *practice*. I mean practice in the sense that it is given by practice theorists like Pierre Bourdieu and Sherry Ortner, namely, that human actions (practices) are best understood as strategic methods for getting things done while working within the constraints of existing power structures. Practice, as an analytical category, focuses attention on the strategic, productive, politically invested, and ultimately self-interested aspects of human activity. Most theorists of ritual today adopt the solution to the problem of reification proposed by Catherine Bell in *Ritual Theory, Ritual Practice*. Bell treats ritual as just another thing that people do. Its significance lies not in its meaning or in its function but in the ways that the people involved in it bend it toward their own self-interest. Ritual, like all practice, is a strategic means of using the body to achieve a particular goal.[18]

Given the influence of Bell's ideas in contemporary ritual studies, it is impossible to teach a course on ritual without teaching practice theory. That does not necessitate that it be one of the core ideas underlying the course, as I have made it. I organized my course around practice because it has become one of the most important analytical categories in virtually all social scientific fields. Students who have internalized the concept of practice will find that it makes anthropology, sociology, history, political science, economics, and a host of other disciplines intelligible to them. Practice, like reification, thus promotes interdisciplinarity. Like reification, it also promotes cultural competency and global/local awareness. Practice is a universal concept, applicable to any human community in time and space; however, discrete practices, because they are strategic and goal-oriented, are intelligible only when considered against the backdrop of their complete sociocultural contexts.

### Essential Questions

Working backward from the ideas *reification* and *practice*, I formulated two essential questions to orient course content: (1) "To what extent are we conscious of the reasons for the things that we do?" and (2) "Is ritual a thing?"

According to Wiggins and McTighe, essential questions can take one of two forms. They can be *overarching* questions that cross the boundaries of units, courses, and academic disciplines, or they can be narrower, *topical* questions.[19] Although Wiggins and McTighe suggest framing essential questions for a course as overarching questions, I chose to frame my ritual course around one overarching question and one (very broad) topical question. The overarching question ("To what extent are we conscious of the reasons for the things that we do?"), I derived primarily from the concept of practice. This question arises naturally out of any interaction with practice theory. According to practice theorists, we are rarely, if ever, fully

18. Bell, *Ritual Theory*, passim. Bell argues that practice theory is able to transcend the dichotomies of thought versus action, universal versus particular, and observer versus participant by locating them in the body and in its accumulated and internalized habits. Ritual is not the acting out of prior thoughts because thought is itself a mode of bodily action; thus ritual cannot be observed by the scholar as a site that makes belief intelligible.
19. Wiggins and McTighe, *Understanding by Design*, 114–15.

aware of the reasons for our actions. In fact, we are frequently apt to misrecognize the self-interest inherent in our actions. The question is also, however, closely intertwined with the study of ritual: in the popular imagination (and often in the scholarly imagination as well), ritual is regarded as formulaic, mindless, and automatic, the opposite of intentional, strategic action. Framing a course on ritual around the question of agency and intentionality lays the groundwork for us to challenge that stereotype.

In addition to the overarching question of why we do things, the course was also framed around a topical question that arose naturally from the problem of reification: "Is ritual a thing?" I chose to frame this question topically because my attempts at reframing it in overarching terms grew unwieldy in their abstraction: "In what inheres the thingness of things?," "What constitutes the substance of a social fact?," and the like. Wiggins and McTighe suggest, however, that essential questions ought to be questions that come up naturally in the course of our lives.[20] "Is ritual a thing?" does not come up naturally very often, but we often ask, in the course of everyday conversation, "Is that a thing now?" The question connects the cultural moment to current academic debate: its phrasing picks up on the ways that people actually talk to each other right now, and its substance invokes an unsettled dispute among scholars in ritual studies. It naturally piques students' curiosity, and it gives them a sense of what is actually at stake in the academic discussion.

These questions, finally, are both genuinely open-ended: a wide range of opinions on both issues can be found within current scholarly literature. My mind is not made up about either of them. That is, perhaps, the most important factor. While it is possible for a good teacher to create a space of genuine open-endedness around a topic that she has made up her mind about, in practice students often end up internalizing the prejudices of their teacher. That is why I try, as much as I can, to frame my courses around questions that I have not answered, even provisionally, to my own satisfaction.[21] It decenters the classroom. We become a learning community in search of a common goal: our own distinctive understandings of the big ideas behind these essential questions.

## Enduring Understandings

To promote the open-endedness of classroom discourse, I framed the enduring understandings that represent the specific goals for my course as propositions that respond to the essential questions. They are not definitive answers that I expect students to memorize and regurgitate; rather, they represent provisional answers, advanced by experts in the field of ritual studies, which we will attempt to evaluate

---

20. Ibid., 108.
21. On the importance that essential questions always be open questions, see ibid., 121–24. For similar articulations specifically within the field of religious studies, see Jonathan Z. Smith, "'Narratives into Problems': The College Introductory Course and the Study of Religion," *JAAR* 56, no. 4 (1988): 727–39, and Natalie Gummer, "A Profound Unknowing: The Challenge of Religion in the Liberal Education of World Citizens," *Perspectives* (Spring 2005): 44–49.

over the course of the semester.[22] Students may or may not agree, in the end, with these propositions. That is not important. What matters, rather, is that they understand why they reach whatever conclusion they reach. The propositions that we evaluated in the course were:

- All human action (including ritual) is goal-oriented, whether explicitly or implicitly, and is ultimately self-interested, though human actors are not always aware of their ultimate goals or motives.

- Ritual is a thing when the people doing the rituals identify them as rituals; ritual is also a useful heuristic category when people do not identify their actions as rituals.

Each of these propositions reflects the defining features of understandings in UbD: each is an informed generalization about specific things; each is anchored in a transferable core idea; each is abstract and somewhat counterintuitive; and each involves critical judgment about the applicability of skills and facts in specific contexts that can only be acquired through an extensive process of "uncovering."[23]

Understandings are general and abstract, but that does not mean that they exist independently of the content that they elucidate. Rather, in the UbD template, understandings are strategies for selecting and organizing course content so that it is meaningful to students. Per the UbD template, I used the enduring understandings articulated above as a "filter" for determining which aspects of ritual theory to cover in the course. Space prohibits a comprehensive account of the knowledge and skills covered in the course, so I will focus on the most pervasive. Since we are concerned with whether or not ritual is a "thing," we must have a sense of the characteristics of ritual-like behavior that people frequently use to identify ritual as such, and we must have a working typology of ritual genres. Since we are concerned with the inherently interested and goal-oriented dimensions of human action, we need to know what the people performing ritualized actions understand themselves to be doing, and we need to know the actual effects of their actions. This necessitates that we study the contexts in which rituals are performed. Finally, because the reification of ritual is a function of past scholarly discussions, we need to know what past thinkers have said about ritual so that we know what is at stake in the current debate.

## Assessment

It was at this stage in the design process, after I had pinpointed enduring understandings and the specific content that would support them, that I began thinking seriously about assessments. Wiggins and McTighe note that the assessment stage is where the UbD template seems especially counterintuitive to many teachers.[24]

---

22. See Wiggins and McTighe, *Understanding by Design*, 132–33, esp. on the distinction between facts and understandings, and on the "expert blind spot."
23. See ibid., 129–30. Note that I have folded the last two dimensions of the definition of understanding in UbD into a single statement.
24. Ibid., 146, 150–52.

We are conditioned to resist the idea that we should "teach to the test," since that appears to devalue the intrinsic interest that students are supposed to develop for the material. Instead, we generate content on the basis of our expertise in the topic, and then we design assessments that test what we taught our students. The UbD template, however, insists that we generate both content and assessments on the basis of core ideas, essential questions, and enduring understandings. The idea is that, if you design assessments that actually tests students' conceptual understanding of core ideas, you can and should "teach to the test."

The trick is designing assessments that test more than content recall. I have always been frustrated by the gap between my students' classroom experience and their performance on assessments. According to Wiggins and McTighe, assessment should be designed to provide evidence that students have acquired the understandings articulated in the first stage of the design process. At the highest level, I wanted students to understand that all human action is potentially goal-oriented and that ritual is both a substantive and an analytical category, depending on the context. How do students demonstrate that they understand those concepts? I immediately rejected the notion of providing assessments that ask those questions directly because I feared that students would simply parrot what they perceived to be *my* understanding without adequately demonstrating *their* understandings.[25] Rather, I thought it was crucial that they develop these understandings intuitively, through repeated exposure to the underlying ideas and through multiple opportunities to apply these ideas in practice. Moreover, Wiggins and McTighe argue that authenticity is crucial to assessment, meaning that assessments must provide students with opportunities to demonstrate their ability to apply the right knowledge in realistically imagined contexts.[26] Authentic assessment of students' understanding of anything related to ritual would demand that they both observe rituals and perform them.

I settled on two assessments that would target these higher-level understandings. First, students would be required to write three short (four-to-six pages) papers analyzing rituals that they had observed or read about.[27] They would be required to observe one ritual in person, and they would be required to analyze no more than one ritual from their own faith tradition. They would be asked to describe the ritual, including an account of how they observed it or otherwise came to know about it. They would also be required to provide information on the ritual's context. Is it part of a larger ritual complex? Where is the ritual situated within the life of the community, past and present? Finally, they would be required to analyze the ritual, focusing especially on its outcomes, and distinguishing between participants' assessments and their own assessments.

For the second assignment testing higher-level understandings, students would be required to divide into self-selected small groups and design rituals to be performed in class. I requested that the ritual performances be inclusive and nonsectarian, such that all students in theory be able to participate. Otherwise, I gave them significant latitude. The group would be required to submit a short paper

25. See, again, Wiggins and McTighe on the "expert blind spot," in ibid., 132–33.
26. Ibid., 153–54.
27. See exhibit 6 in the appendix, below, for an example of this rubric.

analyzing their own ritual according to the same criteria for the first assignment; other students would be required to do the same twice during the semester.

Both assignments also required students to apply their lower-level knowledge of the characteristics and genres of ritual-like actions and of various ritual theorists. Without this knowledge, higher-level understandings are impossible, and the papers provided students with opportunities to demonstrate not only that they had learned these facts but that they could transfer that knowledge to new contexts. To reinforce this knowledge, I assigned them six open-book online quizzes that would ask straightforward content questions about the readings. Through these quizzes, students could demonstrate, at a basic level, their competence with the building blocks of ritual theory.

The final, and most heavily weighted, arena for assessment was class participation. I had the luxury of a small class (twelve students), and I felt confident of my ability to design in-class activities that would allow all students (even the quieter ones) to participate. To encourage them to prepare for class, I tied a significant portion of their participation credit to the completion of "focused reading responses," short, informal written responses to the readings that would be turned in before class and incorporated into class discussion. I intended these response papers primarily as an accountability mechanism to ensure that students would be able to engage at a high level during class. Students would receive significant credit simply for participating; full credit would be reserved for those who showed a growing deep-level facility with the understandings behind these questions.

### Curriculum Design

Assessments also dictated curriculum design. Because students needed to learn the basic terminology associated with ritual studies in order to advance toward deeper-level understandings, we started there. This required that we read the assigned textbook, Catherine Bell's *Ritual: Perspectives and Dimensions* (Oxford: Oxford University Press, 2009), out of order. She begins the book with a lengthy discussion of the history of ritual theory as an academic discipline; I felt, however, that students would need to encounter ritual intuitively at first before they would be able to access more abstract scholarly literature on it. I also wanted them to develop the habit of thinking of ritual as a substantive phenomenon before they began to wrestle in earnest with the issue of reification. We began with a short unit on the basic characteristics of ritual-like action, followed by a unit on genres of ritual. Then we worked diachronically through an exemplary set of theoretical readings. Finally, we returned to the discussion of actual rituals in their deeply embedded sociohistorical contexts, this time bringing our theoretical understandings to bear as well.

### Results

Earlier, I said that my greatest error this semester lay in not committing fully to the UbD template. While I used UbD extensively in designing the syllabus for "Ritual and Ritualization," I abandoned it almost entirely once the fog of war set in: in my preparations for individual class sessions, I reverted almost entirely to the "coverage" model. I prepared exercises (mostly in-class discussions) that highlighted the important points for students to learn from each set of readings, and I invited them to critique the readings in light of other things that they had learned, but I devoted only minimal attention to the core ideas that anchored each course. This particular failure on my part stems largely from the fact that I had not fully internalized the conceptual framework provided by UbD. I treated it as a step-by-step process for simplifying course design. Once the course was designed, I let my prior conceptual framework—that of coverage—dictate lesson planning.

My failure in this respect supports UbD as a teaching paradigm. Students learn whatever course design emphasizes. In this case, my students became quite proficient at identifying the core characteristics and genres of ritual-like action because we introduced these first and reinforced them consistently throughout the semester. Students' understanding of the concepts of *practice* and *reification*, however, was limited, in large part because I did not emphasize either concept until we read an excerpt from Bell's *Ritual Theory, Ritual Practice*, almost two-thirds of the way into the semester. Although we continued to emphasize practice during the final third of the semester, many students struggled to apply it in new settings. Reification, meanwhile, was only explicitly discussed on the last day of class. Students were caught off-guard by it. I had expected that a course designed around core ideas and enduring understandings would naturally reinforce those things. I failed to reinforce them actively throughout the semester, and students reflected that failure in their learning outcomes. Instead, I should have designed each class session around a set of learning outcomes that related, in some way, to these core ideas.

## Course #2: Space and Place in Early Judaism

I chose to teach this course in large part because it reflects my research interests: my dissertation uses critical spatial theory as an interpretive lens for reading the biblical book of Ezra-Nehemiah. I quickly discovered, however, that my expertise in the field presented its own problems. I am committed to structuring courses around open-ended questions that I have not resolved to my own satisfaction. In my research, I adopt firm positions about most of the major issues in my subfield. That doesn't mean my positions are the right ones, despite my best efforts (and my worst pretensions), but it does mean that my students can only authentically challenge my positions if they acquire a commensurate level of knowledge, something that the language barrier alone precludes (none of them knows biblical Hebrew). Decentering the classroom in this context requires that we shift the terms of discussion backward a step, to larger-scale conceptual issues that are open-ended for all of us. Ideally, I wanted to level the playing field by creating a framework where students' subjective, situated responses to the text could be raised up for analysis and integrated into the overall discussion.

## Big Ideas

I settled on two core ideas for the class: place and identity.[28] Neither relates explicitly to Judaism or to Judean literature,[29] but both can be used to frame essential questions about ancient Judeans and their complex relationship with the world in which they lived. Both concepts, moreover, can readily be used to interrogate our own experiences. We often take the relationship between place and identity for granted. Simply by calling it into question, we unsettle ourselves in our world. This is because, experientially, place is an anchor-point, a strategy for orienting ourselves within the cosmos. We think of place as something that shapes us; in practice, the process is much more dialectical. The places in which we find ourselves today are often radically different from those that shaped the identities of early Judeans, but the basic strategies by which we emplace ourselves in our world are shared by all humans in time and space. When we recognize the ways that we construct our own worlds, we become better able to relate to the ways that other people have done the same thing in their own contexts.

Although the title of the course is "Space and Place in Early Judaism," I chose to focus on place for one simple reason: in experiential terms, place is primary. In humanistic geography, the terms *place* and *space* represent opposite poles on a continuum between (respectively) boundedness and openness, differentiation and chaos, security and freedom, fixity and motion.[30] Experientially, though, place comes first. We do not enter into place and then begin to experience it. There is no experience apart from place and the constitutive influence that it exerts on our senses.[31] The body does not merely exist in place; it exists as part of place, and when it moves it takes place with itself. Space, by contrast, is a theoretical abstraction, a concept that we use to describe what lies between discrete places. What we call "space" from a phenomenological perspective is the sort of place where the undifferentiated and unfamiliar crowds close against the place of the body, the primal place that anchors subjectivity.[32] Place, almost by definition, is where the body can be situated among what is familiar.[33]

The other big idea at the core of the course was identity. Because place and the body are co-constitutive of one another, identity is necessarily deeply enmeshed in both. For the purpose of this class, I chose to treat identity not as an analytical

28. On "core ideas" and other UbD terminology throughout this section, see the previous section, "Course #1: Ritual and Ritualization."

29. On the use of the term *Judean*, see Steve Mason, "Judaeans, Judaizing, Judaism: Problems of Categorization in Ancient History," *Journal for the Study of Judaism* 38, nos. 4-5 (2007): 457–512.

30. Anne Buttimer, "Phenomenology, Existentialism, and the Study of Values," in *Values in Geography*, Commission on College Geography Resource Paper 24 (Washington, DC: Association of American Geographers, 1974); Edward Relph, *Place and Placelessness*, Research in Planning and Design (London: Routledge, 1976); Yi-Fu Tuan, *Space and Place: The Perspective of Experience* (Minneapolis: University of Minnesota Press, 1977); Edward Casey, *Getting Back into Place: Toward a Renewed Understanding of the Place-World*, 2d ed. (Bloomington: Indiana University Press, 2009).

31. Casey, *Getting Back into Place*, 317–19.

32. Ibid., 50–55; Smith, *To Take Place*, 26–35.

33. Casey, *Getting Back into Place*, 24–25.

category but, rather, as a category of practice.[34] This means that, rather than theorizing the term extensively and defining it concretely, I used the term as my students use it in their everyday lives, and I let the interaction between identities and places (both ancient and modern) determine how we thought about identity in the classroom. As an icebreaker on the first day of class, for instance, we discussed how our hometowns had influenced our identities. Students talked about how their hometowns had shaped their personalities, their religious beliefs, their taste in food and music, their political orientations, among other things. Identity, in this flexible and practical sense, can be transferred to the ancient world in the context of the classroom: it becomes a means to ask who someone is, and who they think they are.[35]

## Essential Questions and Enduring Understandings

I wanted to structure the course around my students' encounter with people who were very different from themselves, even when Jewishness itself is shared in common. Therefore, I selected one overarching question and one topical question, each of which in turn generated corresponding overarching and topical understandings. First, the overarching question: "How do place and identity interact with each other?" This question generated the following understanding: "Place is deeply interconnected with identity on physical, conceptual, and experiential levels in intricately complex ways." By invoking the triad of physical, conceptual, and experiential spatialities, I sought to connect the course to critical spatial theory, where the triad is commonplace.[36] According to some theorists, physical space refers to space as it can be studied empirically and objectively; conceptual space refers to mental representations of space, often as reflected in discourse (whether spoken or written), and experiential space refers to the lived interaction between physical and conceptual spaces. I wanted to make sure that students understood that space and place are not merely physical in nature; their meaning is also bound up in how people think about them and interact with them. By invoking complexity, meanwhile, I wanted to reinforce that places can exist on a full range of geographical

---

34. On this distinction, see Rogers Brubaker and Frederick Cooper, "Beyond 'Identity,'" *Theory and Society* 29, no. 1 (2000): 1–47. Brubaker and Cooper argue that scholars should dispense with the term *identity* as an analytical concept: on the one hand, identity has been defined so broadly in scholarly literature that it has almost no meaning outside of its immediate context, and, on the other hand, it has also been reified outside of scholarly discourse, such that its continued usage as an analytical category reinforces its perception as a substantive entity. We are better off, Brubaker and Cooper argue, choosing more precise analytical terms and using *identity* as it is used in the contexts in which it is found.

35. Schatzki distinguishes between *meaning* (i.e., what something is) and *identity* (who someone is, in their own articulation); both are functions of a person's position within the broader social structure of orders and practices. I accept Schatzki's distinction, but I did not use it in class for the sake of simplicity. See Theodore R. Schatzki, *The Site of the Social: A Philosophical Account of the Constitution of Social Life and Change* (University Park: Pennsylvania State University Press, 2002), 47, 53–56.

36. Henri Lefebvre, *The Production of Space*, trans. Donald Nicholson-Smith (Cambridge: Blackwell, 1991); David Harvey, *The Condition of Postmodernity: An Enquiry into the Origins of Cultural Change* (Hoboken, NJ: Wiley-Blackwell, 1989); Edward W. Soja, *Thirdspace: Journeys in Los Angeles and Other Real-and-Imagined Places* (Cambridge: Blackwell, 1996).

scales, from the body to globe, and that people, as individuals and as groups, have distinctive ways of understanding these places' meanings. I wanted students to try to wrap their minds around the sheer enormity of all of the possible places and all of the possible conceptions of those places.

The topical question that anchored the course was an application of the overarching understanding of place and identity: "Given the intricate relationship between place and identity, how did ancient Judeans respond to the conditions of exile, diaspora, deportation, and colonial subjugation, and how did their responses shape their identities?" The following topical understanding arose from that question: "Place-making strategies were crucial to the survival, perpetuation, and shaping of Judean culture, particularly as Judeans developed ways to make sacred space portable." By focusing on strategies, I wanted students to understand that the wildly diverse conceptions of space and place that we encountered in early Judean texts resulted from actual Judeans articulating their own notions of their worlds, and I wanted students to be able to trace the substantive differences between these competing Judaic worlds. By focusing on survival and perpetuation, meanwhile, I wanted students to see that, unlike most of the petty kingdoms of the ancient Levant, Judah generated an enduring (and, via Christianity and Islam, a wildly expansive) genealogy of religious traditions. I proposed *place-making* to my students as an analytical lens for understanding, at least in part, why history developed in such a way that Judaism exists in the world today.

### Knowledge and Skills

In order for students to attain these understandings and demonstrate their competence in them, I determined that they'd need to acquire knowledge and skills in three broad areas. First, they would need some knowledge of history, geography, and culture relative to early Judean society. I did not want the class to turn into a "survey" course, so I attempted to filter this content to include only what they would need to know to engage meaningfully with the texts we would be reading. For that reason, I chose to assign Martin Jaffee's *Early Judaism: Religious Worlds of the First Judaic Millennium* (2d ed.; Bethesda: University Press of Maryland, 2006). It covers the proper time period (c. 500 BCE—c. 500 CE), it provides a level of content knowledge appropriate to an introductory course, and it organizes that content thematically rather than chronologically. This last point is crucial: I wanted to organize the course around the comparison of conceptual Judean spatialities (as expressed in ancient Judean texts) so as to avoid the implication that early Judean history inevitably culminates with the rabbinic movement.

In addition to this content-specific knowledge, the textual focus of the course necessitated that students learn how to read ancient texts with sensitivity, nuance, and caution. They needed, on the one hand, to understand that these texts reflect radically different presuppositions about reality than anything that has been written in the postmodern West; but, on the other hand, they also needed to be able to engage with the texts and to relate to the people who produced them. I am trained as a biblical scholar, so I am eminently well-qualified to model these skills in the classroom (or at least I ought to be!). For that reason, I chose to assign only a small number of academic articles on ancient Judean literature,[37] and to focus instead on reading through primary sources directly.

Finally, students would need significant exposure to critical spatial theory. Academic literature on critical spatiality is notoriously dense and abstract, so I decided to put off introducing students to it until they had already acquired most of the necessary content-area knowledge and exegetical acumen that the course would require. During the first half of the course, I had them read through the textbook, and I assigned relevant primary texts to support it. After the midterm break, I assigned them an introductory reading on cultural geography, followed by a series of theoretical articles and chapters on critical spatiality. I juxtaposed these theoretical readings provocatively against primary texts in the hope that class time would be used to explore the spatial dynamics of ancient Judean writings.

## Assessments

There are ways to test each of these sets of knowledge and skills individually, and I considered assigning regular quizzes and midterm exams to cover the content-area knowledge. However, I ultimately decided that the evidence of understanding that I valued most was my students' ability to use their knowledge of spatial theory to arrive at sensitive, meaningful readings of ancient Judean texts. Rather than scaffold that skill set via quizzes, exams, and short exploratory writing prompts, I decided to distribute it evenly across five writing assignments throughout the semester. Each assignment would involve three stages: first, a rough draft; second, a peer review; and, third, a final draft that I would grade.[38] Students were given the opportunity to revise for a higher grade after I graded their work. Each assignment would be built around a prompt that would require students to demonstrate their competence in one or more of the skill areas listed in the previous paragraph. The prompt would also give students tremendous latitude in synthesizing content-area knowledge, exegetical skills, and critical spatial theory.

Crucially, I did not plan the individual prompts out in advance; rather, I crafted them as the semester unfolded. I did this because I wanted to be able to respond to the class's interests over the course of the semester. In this respect, I may have deviated somewhat from the UbD template. Though Wiggins and McTighe allow that the basic steps of UbD may be done in any order,[39] they do insist on a tight congruence between assessment and curriculum. Assessments test understandings; curriculum prepares students for assessments. In my design, by contrast, I based curriculum on my own deep knowledge of early Jewish literature and critical spa-

---

37. Again, the language barrier was a key factor in this decision. Most academic articles on ancient Judean literature presuppose an audience that can read Hebrew, Aramaic, and Greek. Of course, it is possible to scaffold such articles with lists of key terms and definitions, but preparing these documents is often prohibitively labor-intensive.

38. See exhibit 7 in the appendix, below, for an example of this rubric.

39. Wiggins and McTighe, *Understanding by Design*, 254–74.

tial theory, and I tied assessment to this curriculum, generating writing prompts that I thought would position students to integrate the material on their own terms. I anticipated that students would bring their own experiences to bear on the texts that they were reading and develop their own ways of synthesizing the disparate strands of course content.

## Results

In retrospect, my decision to forgo traditional summative assessments and to craft writing assignments "on the fly" was a major mistake. It violates Jonathan Z. Smith's Iron Law: "A student may not be asked to integrate what the faculty will not."[40] Because assessments were not tied *in specific ways* to both enduring understandings and day-to-day curriculum, the course became frustratingly episodic. Because students knew that they would not be tested on content, they had little incentive to prioritize learning it, apart from what was needed for in-class discussions and for their specific papers. Because the assignments themselves were self-contained and there was no culminating summative assessment, students were not formally encouraged to engage in large-scale synthesis. Some of the individual papers were exceptionally good, and a couple of the students in the class showed improvement in their writing over the course of the semester, but few of the papers displayed a deep-level understanding of spatiality or of ancient Judaism. In retrospect, I should have cut down on the number of writing assignments and provided midterm and final summative assessments that required students to demonstrate a synthetic understanding of course content, and I should have used the writing assignments to invite students to explore that synthesis on their own terms.

Despite these shortcomings, the course was largely a success. Students seem to have enjoyed it, and in the process they produced some very good writing. The course fell somewhat short of its full potential, however, and it produced little in the way of enduring understanding, particularly with respect to ancient Judaism. I must stress: this is *my* fault. Students cannot be expected to integrate everything in a course into their limited set of enduring understandings, and I had given them no reason to prioritize one set of ideas over any other. Individual class sessions were often tremendously engaging: students did the reading and argued about its significance in ways that suggested that they found the course very interesting. Unfortunately, I saw scant evidence that they were developing higher-level synthetic understandings of the material.

## What I Learned from Using UbD

As a biblical scholar teaching outside of the field of biblical studies, I found UbD indispensable for its ability to help me to isolate coherent sets of core ideas in

---

40. Jonathan Z. Smith, "Re-forming the Undergraduate Curriculum: A Retrospective," in Lehrich, ed., *On Teaching Religion*, 93–110, here 94. Smith goes on to state that "By charter, by statute, by any notion of faculty responsibility, not to speak of by student fee, it is the faculty *alone* who is charged with providing organization" (emphasis original).

disciplines like ritual studies and Jewish studies. Though the UbD template is intended to facilitate deep-level understandings for students, it also helps to expedite the process for the teacher. The prospect of "covering" an unfamiliar discipline is daunting, almost paralyzing; UbD, by shifting the focus to "uncovering," frees the teacher to narrow the discipline down to a limited number of core ideas that, in turn, make a large portion of its literature intelligible. These ideas cannot be determined arbitrarily; neither, however, do they need to be all-encompassing.

The UbD template, by insisting on the importance of organizing a whole course around a limited set of core ideas, has also helped me to approach courses in my own field. The prospect of "doing justice" to the full breadth of my knowledge of biblical studies can be just as daunting as the prospect of learning a new field of study. Indeed, it can be worse: in my own discipline, I know full well all that I am skipping! Moreover, by encouraging me to design my courses around questions that I have not settled to my own satisfaction, I hope that UbD will help me to avoid falling into the habit of simply telling students what I know. By conceptualizing every course session as a piece of a puzzle whose final form I have not seen in full, I shift the heaviest intellectual lifting to my students without abdicating my obligation to provide a basic level of synthesis. Therein lies the difference between "open-ended" and "without direction."

Next semester, I am teaching two classes, "Geography of Religion" and "Gender and Sexuality in Rabbinic Judaism." I will be designing both courses from scratch, and I have already committed fully to the UbD template for this task. Indeed, the most important lesson I have taken away from the previous semester is to treat UbD less as like a process and more like a conceptual framework. Thus, I will be making two changes in the approach that I used for "Ritual and Ritualization" and "Space and Place in Early Judaism." First, I will use UbD not only to design my syllabi but also to plan my individual lessons throughout the semester. I will attempt to tie every class session to the big ideas and enduring understandings that anchor the course as a whole. Second, I will also tie these individual sessions to my assessments. I will commit fully to "teaching to the test," with the qualification that these assessments enable students to demonstrate their deep-level understanding of the course's core ideas. I have high hopes that this approach will help to improve one of the things that has frustrated me most about my teaching in the past: the gap between my students' enthusiasm for individual class sessions and their performance on exams and papers.

## Works Cited

Asad, Talal. *Genealogies of Religion: Discipline and Reasons of Power in Christianity and Islam*. Baltimore: Johns Hopkins Press, 1993.

Bell, Catherine. *Ritual Theory, Ritual Practice*. New York: Oxford University Press, 1992.

———. *Ritual: Perspectives and Dimensions*. Oxford: Oxford University Press, 1997.

Brubaker, Rogers, and Frederick Cooper. "Beyond 'Identity.'" *Theory and Society* 29, no. 1 (2000): 1–47.

Buttimer, Anne. "Phenomenology, Existentialism, and the Study of Values." In *Values in Geography*. Commission on College Geography Resource Paper 24. Washington, DC: Association of American Geographers, 1974.

Casey, Edward. *Getting Back into Place: Toward a Renewed Understanding of the Place-World*. 2d ed. Bloomington: Indiana University Press, 2009.

Freire, Paolo. *Pedagogy of the Oppressed*. Trans. Myra Bergman Ramos. New York: Continuum, 1993.

Gummer, Natalie. "A Profound Unknowing: The Challenge of Religion in the Liberal Education of World Citizens." *Perspectives* (Spring 2005): 44–49.

Harvey, David. *The Condition of Postmodernity: An Enquiry into the Origins of Cultural Change*. Hoboken, NJ: Wiley-Blackwell, 1989.

Lefebvre, Henri. *The Production of Space*. Trans. Donald Nicholson-Smith. Cambridge: Blackwell, 1991.

Lofton, Kathryn. Review of J. Z. Smith and C. I. Lehrich, *On Teaching Religion*. *Journal of the American Academy of Religion* 82 (2014): 531–42.

Mason, Steve. "Judaeans, Judaizing, Judaism: Problems of Categorization in Ancient History." *Journal for the Study of Judaism* 38, nos. 4-5 (2007): 457–512.

"The Oxford Dictionaries Word of the Year Is . . ." *Oxford Dictionaries*. http://blog.oxford-dictionaries.com/2013/11/word-of-the-year-2013-winner/.

*Oxford English Dictionary*. 3d ed. Oxford: Oxford University Press, 2014.

"Religious Studies." Beloit College. http://www.beloit.edu/religious/.

Relph, Edward. *Place and Placelessness*. Research in Planning and Design. London: Routledge, 1976.

Schatzki, Theodore R. *The Site of the Social: A Philosophical Account of the Constitution of Social Life and Change*. University Park: Pennsylvania State University Press, 2002.

"Selfie." Wikipedia. http://en.wikipedia.org/wiki/Selfie.

Smith, Jonathan Z. *To Take Place: Toward Theory in Ritual*. Chicago Studies in the History of Judaism. Chicago: University of Chicago Press, 1987.

———. "'Narratives into Problems': The College Introductory Course and the Study of Religion." *Journal of the American Academy of Religion* 56, no. 4 (1988): 727–39.

———. "Introduction: Approaching the College Classroom." In *On Teaching Religion*, 1–8. Ed. C. I. Lehrich. New York: Oxford University Press, 2013.

———. "Re-forming the Undergraduate Curriculum: A Retrospective." In *On Teaching Religion*, 93–110. Ed. C. I. Lehrich. New York: Oxford University Press, 2013.

Soja, Edward W. *Thirdspace: Journeys in Los Angeles and Other Real-and-Imagined Places*. Cambridge: Blackwell, 1996.

"Top Ten Everything of 2012." *Time*. http://newsfeed.time.com/2012/12/04/top-10-news-lists/slide/selfie/.

Tuan, Yi-Fu. *Space and Place: The Perspective of Experience*. Minneapolis: University of Minnesota Press, 1977.

Wiggins, Grant, and Jay McTighe. *Understanding by Design*. Exp. 2nd ed. Alexandria, VA: Association for Supervision and Curriculum Development, 2005.

# Appendix

**F**undamental to Understanding by Design (UbD) is an ideal of transparency: learners should know what big ideas animate the course, and what enduring understandings we hope for them to arrive at. When undertaking their course work, learners should know as much as possible about how the work will be assessed.

While assessment rubrics, as such, are not a formal part of UbD, the contributors to this volume have found them invaluable in accomplishing this ideal of transparency. In this appendix are compiled assessment rubrics corresponding to the courses we describe in the body of the book. An excellent, practical introduction to rubrics is widely recognized in Dannelle D. Stevens and Antonia Levi, *Introduction to Rubrics: An Assessment Tool to Save Grading Time, Convey Effective Feedback, and Promote Student Learning*, 1st ed. (Sterling, VA: Stylus), 2005.

## Exhibits

The following "exhibits" are referenced in the book.

Exhibit 1: *Rubric for Presentations* (Lester); footnote, p. 44.

Exhibit 2: *All-Purpose Rubric for "Introduction to the Old Testament"* (Lester); footnote, p. 57.

Exhibit 3: *Annotated Sample Template for Essay in "New Testament"* (Webster); in-line, pp. 82-84.

Exhibit 4: *Interdisciplinary Institutional Rubric for Writing at Barton College* (Webster); footnote, p. 85.

Exhibit 5: *Rubric for Essays in "New Testament"* (Webster); p. 89.

Exhibit 6: *Rubric for Ritual Analysis Papers in "Ritual and Ritualization"* (Jones); footnote, p.107.

Exhibit 7: *Rubric for Drafts in "Space and Place in Early Jewish Literature"* (Jones); footnote, p. 113.

## *Exhibit 1: Rubric for Presentations (Lester)*

| | Excellent: 100% | Competent: 80% | Developing: 60% | |
|---|---|---|---|---|
| **Content: Understanding and Knowledge** | Presenter controls a narrative, presenting material in logical, interesting sequence. Knowledge is accurate and shows synthesis and texture. | Presenter struggles to convey narrative; or, shows slightly inaccurate or superficial knowledge of material. | Material is disjointed or disorganized, or presenter shows substantive misunderstanding of subject matter. | 20 |
| **Content: Comprehensive Coverage** | Presenter offers a proportional, well-balanced introduction of material and issues. | Presentation misses or marginalizes some key elements of material. | Presentation is markedly nonproportional to subject matter. | 20 |
| **Skills: Verbal** | Presenter uses clear voice, audible volume, correct pronunciation, variety, and adequately slow pace. | Presenter struggles with some aspects: clarity, volume, correctness, variety, or pace. | Presenter mumbles, or races, or speaks too softly to be heard, or mispronounces key terms. | 20 |
| **Skills: Non-Verbal** | Presenter maintains continuing eye contact, relaxed movements, positive attitude toward subject matter. | Presenter struggles with some aspects: eye contact, relaxed movements, or positive attitude toward subject matter. | Presenter makes little eye contact, or is distractingly ill at ease, or shows negative or indifferent attitude toward subject matter. | 20 |
| **A/V elements** | Graphics follow spirit of "20/20" and "1/1/5," supporting and reinforcing presenter, with professional mechanics. | Graphics sporadically follow spirit of "20/20" and "1/1/5," or occasionally distract from presenter's narrative, or fall short in some mechanics. | Text predominates the A/V elements, or are poorly balanced/paced, or poor spelling/ other mechanics are apparent. | 20 |
| **SUM TOTAL** | | | | 100 |

## Exhibit 2: All-Purpose Rubric for "Introduction to the Old Testament" (Lester)

|  | Excellent (25) | Competent (20) | Unsatisfactory (15) |  |
|---|---|---|---|---|
| **Completeness** | The work fully develops every aspect of the assignment, and the organization of the work makes this easy to see. | The work appears to develop each aspect of the assignment, though this is hard to discern clearly at points. | The work does not fully develop every aspect of the assignment. | 25 |
| **Exegesis and Hermeneutics** | The work has clear focus on meaning of text(s) for likely authors in their own historical/social contexts, as well as distinct focus on possible meanings for explicitly described modern readers. | The work has clear focus on meaning of text(s) for likely authors in their own historical/ social contexts. May have unclear but discernible focus on possible meanings for modern readers. | The work lacks clear focus on meaning of text(s) for likely authors in their own historical/ social contexts. | 25 |
| **Engage Course Materials** | The work substantively engages, in accurate detail, the material of our shared coursework (readings, lectures, discussion). The course materials make a substantive difference to the work. | The work substantively engages the material of our shared coursework: readings, lectures, discussion. At points this engagement is superficial or inaccurate. | The work inadequately engages the material of our shared coursework. | 25 |
| **Engage Course Big Ideas & Essential Questions** | The work substantively engages the "big ideas" and "essential questions" of the course. | The work engages the "big ideas" and "essential questions," while this engagements is at some points unclear or superficial. | The work does not substantively engage the "big ideas" and "essential questions" of the course. | 25 |
|  |  |  |  |  |
| **SUM TOTAL** |  |  |  | 100 |

## Exhibit 4: Interdisciplinary Institutional Rubric for Writing at Barton College (Webster)

| | 1 Unsatisfactory | 2 Developing | 3 Satisfactory | 4 Exemplary |
|---|---|---|---|---|
| **Mechanics (#s per page)** | More than 3 major errors in grammar and/or unclear sentences per page; common, repetitive spelling errors | More than 3 awkward sentences; more than 3 grammatical or spelling errors; inappropriate word choice (e.g., slang, abbreviations, contractions); lack of clarity | Clear sentence structure; no more than 3 minor errors in grammar and spelling; appropriate word choice | Clear and varied sentence structure; almost no errors in grammar and spelling; effective, appropriate word choice |
| **Organization/Structure** | Unclear or absent thesis; lacks clear organization or paragraphing; weak transitions between ideas; lacks introduction and/or conclusion | Basic thesis and organization; most paragraphs have topic sentences; some transitions; weak introduction and/or conclusion | Interesting thesis; clear, logical organization; good transitions; paragraphs support topic sentences; introduction foreshadows arguments and conclusion reviews | Intelligent thesis; smooth, effective organization and transitions; well-designed paragraphs; introduction indicates understanding of topic; conclusion suggests questions or implications. |
| **Content** | Only surface descriptive and/or faulty logic or analysis; overlooks major parts of the topic; evidence missing or unconnected to the argument | Mainly descriptive with some analysis and connections; one-sided or biased; evidence is linked to the argument; covers the topic | Analyzes and evaluates logically; effective use of evidence; treats different points of view fairly; generally convincing | Synthesizes, analyzes and evaluates logically; ample evidence; extends and explores context and/or implications; persuasive |
| **Archival/internet/library research (if required)** | Uses incorrect or only general or basic information; depends on unreliable sources; shows little understanding that sources have a point of view; misquotes and/or almost copies | Uses one-sided or too few sources; most information is accurate; some understanding of sources' arguments; overuse of long quotations; inadequate paraphrasing. | Uses several sufficient, reliable sources; uses accurate information; understands and analyzes at least one source's argument; quotes, paraphrases accurately | Uses diverse sources demonstrating thorough research; analyzes and synthesizes sources' arguments; smooth, correct integration of quotes and paraphrases |
| **Documentation (if required)** | Major errors in documentation | Some errors in documentation | Minor problems in documentation | Correct documentation |

## Exhibit 5: Rubric for Essays in "New Testament" (Webster)

| Expectation (grade) | Describes (0–70) | | Analyzes the evidence (70–80) | Evaluates within its context (80–90) | Extends to a new context (90–100) |
|---|---|---|---|---|---|
| **Writing Style** | More than 3 unclear sentences and/or more than 3 major spelling or grammatical errors. Personal pronouns are not used. Gender-neutral language is used. | | Some awkward sentences; multiple grammatical or spelling errors. Some informal language. | Clear sentence structure; some minor spelling and grammatical errors. | Varied sentence structure; smooth transitions; virtually no spelling and grammatical errors. |
| **Content and Form** | Primary source essay | One-page paper presents accurate information from the assigned reading only. Lacks clear organization. | Paper is structured to demonstrate analysis. Each paragraph has a clear topic sentence that summarizes the evidence presented within that paragraph. Each paragraph is concluded. There is sufficient evidence (at least 3 points). | Paper is structured to demonstrate evaluation. The introduction clearly states a thesis and briefly previews the argument that will follow. Each topic sentence refers back to the thesis. The conclusion reviews the argument and restates the thesis. Paper identifies both trends and countertrends within the text. | Paper is structured to explore extension. The introduction suggests why this text is important in its larger context by *briefly* comparing it to other texts studied. The conclusion returns to this suggestion and poses a number of questions. Examples: author, purpose, dating, historical context, authority, or social concerns. |
| | Essay with secondary sources | No more than 2 pages, paper accurately describes the content of the assigned reading and uses only basic information from secondary sources. | Integrates *information* from secondary sources. | Describes at least one *argument* from secondary sources that contributes to the thesis. | Addressing the questions raised by extension, the paper describes and evaluates a number of solutions based on research from secondary sources. |

| Citation | All primary and secondary references are cited accurately, formatted, and integrated properly. Proper abbreviations are used. There are no long quotations. Paraphrasing eases sentence structure. There is no evidence of plagiarism. Paper is submitted to Turnitin. | | | | |
|---|---|---|---|---|---|
| | Primary source essay | Only primary sources are used. Secondary sources are not used. | Multiple references to the assigned reading demonstrate depth and range of support. | Multiple references indicate that the whole reading was taken into account, even when it contradicts itself. | Depth, breadth, and complexity of reference citation support extension. |
| | Essay with secondary sources | At least 5 post-1975 non-Internet sources are used. At least one specific commentary is used. | Paper accurately reports information from a range of sources. | Paper reflects diversity of sources (e.g., bias, audience, and opinion) and clearly distinguishes between voices. | Paper accurately reports, evaluates, and challenges a range of sources. Bibliography is properly formatted. |

## *Exhibit 6: Rubric for Ritual Analysis Papers in "Ritual and Ritualization" (Jones)*

**Ritual and Ritualization**
Beloit College RLST 230 01 3B C
Instructor: Christopher M. Jones
**Grading Rubric: Ritual Analysis Papers**

Recommended length: 4–6 pp., double-spaced, 12 pt. standard fonts.

Ritual analysis papers will be graded according to the following criteria. You can structure your paper however you like as long as it includes everything required. Outside research is not required, but you'll probably need to do a little, particularly to describe the ritual's context.

### Description of the Ritual
- How do you know about the ritual? Did you observe it first-hand? Did you interview participants? Did you participate yourself? Did you read about it, and if so, where—in an academic journal article, a popular news magazine, a blog? Did you watch a video of it?
- Who participates in the ritual? Members of a certain organization, culture, or faith tradition? Who is among them—e.g., men only, adults only, elders, children, the infirm? How are participants chosen or excluded?
- What happens during the ritual? What are the roles that people play, and what does each participant do? Where is the ritual performed? What objects are incorporated into it? What is said during the ritual?

### Context of the Ritual
- Is the ritual part of a larger ritual system? Does it occur along with other events (e.g., singing the National Anthem before a football game)?
- Is it unique to a particular culture, organization, or faith tradition? How long has it been practiced? How has it changed over time?
- When is it performed? How often? Is it regular or situational?
- Be sure to highlight any other important background information on the ritual. Use your discretion to decide what counts as "important."

### Analysis of the Ritual
- What type of ritual is it? Start with Bell's categories; if your ritual doesn't fit, provide an alternative category.
- Discuss how the ritual incorporates (or does not incorporate) the various characteristics of ritual that Bell articulates.
- Analyze the symbolism (including objects, words, spaces, and gestures) within the ritual. What does it mean?
- What does the ritual accomplish? What are its intended outcomes? Are there any unintended outcomes, too?

### Style
- Spelling and grammar
- Sentence structure and paragraphing
- Overall clarity and readability

Each of these four criteria will count equally. When grading, I will assign a letter grade for each criterion, and then arrive at the final grade by averaging the four letters. While I am not allowing for revision after the paper is graded, I strongly encourage you to discuss your papers with me before you submit them.

## Exhibit 7: Rubric for Drafts in "Space and Place in Early Jewish Literature" (Jones)

**Space and Place in Early Jewish Literature**
Beloit College RLST 240 02 5T W
Instructor: Christopher M. Jones
**Grading Rubric: Draft Writing**

Grading writing is subjective. In an attempt to trim down the level of subjectivity, I am providing you with exactly the same rubric that I will use as I grade your writing. First, I explain the four criteria that I use to assess writing, and then I provide descriptions of those criteria at various grade levels.

### Criteria

1. Formal. Spelling, grammar, word choice, sentence structure, paragraphing, adherence to genre (where applicable).
2. Mimetic. Correspondence with reality. Are your facts straight? Do you represent the arguments and ideas of other people in terms they would recognize? Is your logic coherent?
3. Rhetorical. Is your writing persuasive? Do you pick the right facts, arrange them in a logical progression, address potential counterarguments, and guide me to your conclusion?
4. Expressive. The most subjective category. Do you have an authentic personal voice? Is your writing engaging? Do you use figurative language, and do you use it appropriately?

### Grading

**A**. Formal: Your spelling and grammar are nearly immaculate. You vary sentence structure, word choice, and paragraph length to maintain the reader's interest. Your writing adheres to genre and uses genre inventively. Mimetic: Your facts are correct and you make appropriate logical inferences between them. You present the ideas of other people accurately, in terms they would recognize, even while critiquing them. Rhetorical: Your writing is persuasive; or, if the assignment is not to persuade, you accomplish your stated purpose. You have a point, and every element in your composition leads toward it in some way. Expressive: I connect with you through your writing. You have a distinctive personal voice that does not get lost in the data and in your engagement with others' ideas. Figurative language suits your purpose.

**B**. Formal: Your spelling and grammar are not perfect, but errors do not significantly undermine your writing. Your sentence structure, paragraph length, and use of genre are somewhat wooden but generally acceptable. Mimetic: You make some factual and logical errors, and you sometimes misrepresent others' ideas. Rhetorical: Your writing is somewhat persuasive. You have a point (more or less), but some of your writing is extraneous to it. Expressive: I connect with you—sort of. Your voice gets lost at times, however. You either (1) do not use much figurative language or (2) you use it inappropriately, such that it distracts from your purpose.

**C**. Formal: Errors in spelling and grammar at times obscure your writing. Your sentences and paragraphs are hard to follow at times. Your writing does not fit the genre. Mimetic: Logical and factual errors undermine your point. You engage straw men rather than presenting others' ideas accurately. Rhetorical: Your writing is unpersuasive. Either you don't have a point or you ramble and lose focus. Expressive: I struggle to connect with you. Your tone is either inconsistent or inappropriate. You don't use figurative language, or you misuse it.

**D**. Formal: Errors in spelling and grammar make your writing nearly unreadable. Your sentences and paragraphs are incoherent. Mimetic: Your facts, logic, and use of others' ideas are objectively wrong.

Rhetorical: You either have no point to make or you ignore your stated purpose. Expressive: I cannot connect with you through your writing due to pervasively inappropriate tone and language.

When I grade your writing, I will assign one letter grade for each criterion. I will arrive at a numerical grade by averaging the four letter grades. For some assignments, I will weight one criterion above the others; if so, I will let you know in the instructions.